P9-DTZ-606

AN ESSAY ON THE
VITA NUOVA

LONDON : GEOFFREY CUMBERLEGE
OXFORD UNIVERSITY PRESS

AN ESSAY ON THE
VITA NUOVA

CHARLES S. SINGLETON

Mills College Library
Withdrawn

Published for the Dante Society

BY THE HARVARD UNIVERSITY PRESS

CAMBRIDGE · MASSACHUSETTS

1949

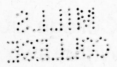
MILLS
COLLEGE

Copyright, 1949
By the President and Fellows of Harvard College
Printed in the United States of America
By the Crimson Printing Company
Cambridge, Massachusetts

851
D192 v.X 2

109170

IN MEMORY OF

ANNIE SOUTHWARD

CONTENTS

AN ESSAY ON THE
VITA NUOVA

There is therefore some other hand that twines the thread of life than that of Nature: we are not only ignorant in antipathies and occult qualities; our ends are as obscure as our beginnings; the line of our days is drawn by night, and the various effects therein by a pencil that is invisible; wherein though we confess our ignorance, I am sure we do not err if we say it is the hand of God.

—Sir Thomas Browne.

Foreword

THE *Vita Nuova* transcends and survives its particular moment in history like any other genuine work of art. But it lacks the great power of the *Divine Comedy*. It will not come all the way to meet us. We must manage to go back *there* if we would see Dante's "sweet little book" for what it is. And, when we do go back, we find ourselves remembering several matters which had long since slipped our minds—matters which are not, as they at first seem to be, so much outside and beyond the *Vita Nuova* as they are outside and beyond the limits of our modern horizon.

Some day it may be the same with a tragedy of Shakespeare. How, for instance, shall *Lear* be tragedy at all unless we remember and remain capable of projecting ourselves into a time when a certain dignity was felt to belong to man and to be guaranteed to him (in some obscure way) by an objective moral order in the cosmos? And yet, as we move further and further away from any general acceptance of such a premise regarding man (witnessed by our inability to produce tragedy in our own "tragic" time), it is not inconceivable that a day may come when as much effort will be demanded of us for the understanding of an Elizabethan tragedy as is now required for a medieval work of art.

Medieval art is, of course, more remote from us now than Shakespeare's. But that is no matter of chronological distance. The tragedy of ancient Greece is closer to us than the art of the Middle Ages. For the latter is a Christian art, its works are profoundly informed with ideas and feelings that are Christian. Nor is this true only of religious art in the Middle Ages. It is true of profane art as well— true, for instance, of the love poetry of the troubadours, even though the love which that poetry celebrated stood judged and condemned in its turn by Christian ideas.

In short, the truth of what Emile Mâle many years ago wrote of the art of the medieval cathedrals has not changed:

The meaning of these profound works gradually became obscure. New generations with a different conception of the world no longer understood them, and from the second half of the sixteenth century medieval art became an enigma. Symbolism, the soul of Gothic art, was dead. . . The Council of Trent marks the end of the old artistic tradition, and we know from a book full of the spirit of the Council that the writer—Molanus the theologian—had lost the key to the art of the Middle Ages.

It happens that the history of the *Vita Nuova* bears striking witness to the truth of these words. A few years after the Council of Trent an edition (the first!) of the *Vita Nuova* appeared in Florence bringing some surprising changes in the text. The word *gloriosa* was changed to *graziosa, beatitudine* to *felicità;* the word *beata* was avoided, and the word *salute* was changed to *quiete*. That is not all. In chapter xxiv the following words were deleted: *però che lo suo nome Giovanna è da quello Giovanni lo quale precedette la verace luce dicendo: Ego vox clamantis in deserto: parate viam Domini.*

What had happened? Exactly what Mâle says had happened. The sixteenth century could no longer see the world as the thirteenth had seen it; consequently, it could take for sacrilege what was only an analogy. Why, for instance, has the editor of 1576 replaced the word *salute* with another? Because he could still hear the burden of its overtone; because, in the way in which the *Vita Nuova* uses the word, he felt that it ought to be said only of Christ—certainly not of a mortal creature, even if her name was *Beatrice*. And in this there is nothing surprising, for Christ, everyone knew, had often been referred to by such a word in Holy Scripture and in the centuries-old gloss to Scripture. Christ is *salus noster*. This editor then was perfectly right in his feeling for the larger meaning of the word, and it is a meaning which we too shall have to recapture if we would see the *Vita Nuova* for what it is. His mistake, however, is to fail to see that, as the *Vita Nuova* has used it, the word declares not an identity but an analogy: an analogy which, understood in its proper medieval terms, is no sacrilege at all. On the contrary, it is *ad majorem Dei gloriam*.

But how shall we see this without readjusting our own eyes to another way of looking at things—eyes which are doubtless more in need of that than those of a sixteenth-century editor. He still felt at least enough about the tone of the word *salute* to take its use in the *Vita Nuova* as an offense against religion. But a reader in the twentieth century is likely to see in that use no more than a playing with words, a pun on the several meanings of *salute:* health, greeting, and salvation.

The changes which time can bring to the public context of his work no artist can foresee. Therefore, he cannot entirely build against this threat from without. When the public context of a work is radically changed or entirely left behind, then the balance of forces which the artist had created between the inside of his work and the outside may be seriously disturbed. For, as he had left it, the inner and private meaning had tension with what was outside, with a context amounting to a kind of public dimension. But when this dimension has changed, that tension is often weakened or lost, what is inner and "private" having no longer anything to play against. This is what has happened to the *Vita Nuova* and, in various measure, to the art of the Middle Ages.

That public dimension of a work of art is, of course, never anywhere except in us. But we have changed very much. For, in the case of medieval art, that dimension in its broadest extension was simply the belief that there is nothing which so much matters in this world as the salvation (*salus*) of the soul—and that through Christ only is true salvation possible.

Now, unless she is seen within the frame of such an idea, what can the meaning of Beatrice be? What can the little world of the *Vita Nuova* mean unless it is rounded (in us) by some sense of that larger world which was standing around it at birth? It is without tension. It no longer meets that resistance from without which the sides of any container make. It goes to pieces and is no longer seen or understood as a living form at all.

The public meaning of *salute* in the *Vita Nuova* is Christ. The private meaning is Beatrice. But without the first, the second, by losing that tension which a work of art can least of all things afford to lose, has lost much more than half of its meaning.

That is why one who desires to understand a work in itself will so often speak of matters which seem to lie outside the work and beyond it. He is concerned with restoring, in whatever degree is still possible, a sense of the form of a work of art. And the problem of interpretation is, as he sees it, merely the problem of relevance tested within the work.

I

The Death of Beatrice

IF Beatrice had not been a miracle, what happened could not have happened.

The signs of the miracle were somewhat obscure at first. One, for instance, was the persistent recurrence of a number nine. But how, in the beginning, was this to be seen for the sign that it really was? The true meaning of such things is made evident only by repetition. Only in retrospect does the sign prove to have been a sign.

The final revelation of miracle came with her death. Then much that had been seen but not understood was made clear: how it was that so many persons had called her *beatrice* without knowing that to be really her name; how it was possible for her greeting to have had the marvelous virtue it had proved to have. She, it was finally clear, was a bringer of beatitude, the beatitude of Heaven. To be sure, she was a woman of flesh and blood, a creature, and mortal even as death had shown. But by this very fact was the greater miracle declared: that mortal creature, a woman, could be the bearer of a beatitude reaching beyond the bounds of nature, reaching back to Heaven because it had come from Heaven. After her death her lover could see the signs for what they were. The number nine had not accompanied Beatrice in life and was not now so emphatically present at her death without some reason. The number had pointed to the true miracle that she was. Anyone at all might see this now—and "now" in the *Vita Nuova* means "now that Beatrice is dead."

It is also in retrospect only that the attentive reader will come to see that the death of Beatrice holds a central position in the *Vita Nuova*. This is true even in point of outward arrangement of the poems. For there are three longer poems so spaced as to mark off the work into three equal parts, and it is the second of these longer

poems, the middle one, which gives us Beatrice dead. We see her dead body. Women are covering her face with a veil. And since the poem is contained in a chapter twenty-three, and since the last chapter of the *Vita Nuova* is numbered forty-two, the death of Beatrice could hardly be more centrally placed.

To a reader familiar with the calculated symmetry of the *Divine Comedy,* such observations will not seem otiose. At a time when this universe of ours revealed to the contemplative eye of man an order and a harmony expressing the substantial order and harmony of its Creator, it cannot be insignificant that the microcosmic vision of a poet should reveal a symmetry resembling that of the greater artifact, the cosmos. Our human art is grandchild to God's. Being this, it can reflect that light by which all that is intelligible comes from Him.

But the death of Beatrice is at the center of the *Vita Nuova* in more than a detail of the surface arrangement of the poems. To a reader in Dante's time it would have been clear from the first words of the book that Beatrice was already dead at the time this was written. He would have known this from a single word in the first sentence of the first chapter of the book proper: from the adjective of the phrase *la gloriosa donna della mia mente.* For the word tells more than any translation can make it tell. It says that, when the author begins his book, Beatrice is already in the glory of eternal life. But even if the modern reader should be insensitive to such delicate connotation, he will not go beyond the following chapter without learning what it had told already. There, when Beatrice first turns her eyes upon the young poet standing fearfully to one side to watch her pass and when she deigns to greet him, she does this, we are told, out of that ineffable courtesy which was hers and which now is rewarded in the world beyond: *meritata nel grande secolo.* And then all readers know that Beatrice is dead.

It is this very fact known from the outset which gives a first glimpse of the form of the *Vita Nuova.* We know at the start that Beatrice is dead. But as we move into the story, we see the little girl dressed in red appear for the first time to the boy who forthwith became her lover. Then we watch her reappear before his eyes to greet him nine years later. And through many events we follow her

to her early death. A circle is complete. At the end we know again
what we knew at the beginning. It is in this sense that the death of
Beatrice is more deeply central to the form of the story, is at its ideal
center, if we may say that beginning and end, when they are the
same, constitute such a center.

By this same circle the poet who is her lover, and whose Book of
Memory this is, becomes as it were two persons, distinguishable according to the principle of time so established. He is the protagonist of the action, moving forward along the line of events in their
first occurrence. And then he is that same person who, having lived
through all these happenings, looks back upon them and sees their
meaning now as it was not possible for him to do at the time. As
the first of these persons he knows nothing before it happens. But
as one reading in a book of memory he knows the end, the middle,
and the beginning of all that happened. This situation in time by
which the poet becomes two persons is of first importance to the
existence of this story as a form. For by that principle a *then* and
a *now* are established for the whole action and, between those two
poles of time, meaning jumps like a spark. Without this condition
in time we cannot have this story. How, for instance, without this
protagonist as he first was, knowing nothing of the end, could the
death of Beatrice break in upon this story with the dramatic suddenness that it has?

He had quite forgotten, it seems, the vision of Beatrice's death
which he had made the subject of the second longer poem. He had
just begun another in celebration of Love's long dominion over him,
when suddenly he knows that she is dead. Solemn words from
Jeremiah announce it to the reader: *Quomodo sedet sola civitas
plena populo! facta est quasi vidua domina gentium.* God has
called the most gentle Beatrice to triumph beneath the banner of
the blessed Queen of Heaven. And the poet cannot even finish the
poem he had begun.

Then, in more ways than one, the poet tells us that the death
of Beatrice was no ordinary death. It was a miracle. One stanza
of that third *canzone* which he now writes says this clearly enough:

Ita n'è Beatrice in l'alto cielo,
   nel reame ove li angeli hanno pace,

e sta con loro, e voi, donne, ha lassate:
no la ci tolse qualità di gelo
nè di calore, come l'altre face,
ma solo fue sua gran benignitate;
chè luce de la sua umilitate
passò li cieli con tanta vertute,
che fè maraviglia l'etterno sire,
sì che dolce disire
lo giunse di chiamar tanta salute;
e fella di qua giù a sè venire,
perchè vedèa ch'esta vita noiosa
non era degna di sì gentil cosa.

Beatrice is gone to the highest heaven, to the realm where the angels find peace, and dwells with them and you, ladies, she has left. No quality of cold nor of heat took her from us as it does other ladies, but it was only her great goodness; for the light of her humility passed through the heavens with so much virtue that it caused the Lord to wonder, so that a sweet desire came upon Him to call such a blessing and He caused her to come from down here to Him because He saw that this noisome life was not worthy of such a gentle thing.

If this were a detached poem, if it had no such context as the *Vita Nuova* gives it, anyone at all familiar with the lyric poetry of Dante's time might discount this claim of miracle as the merest hyperbole of a poet-lover, as a pretty way of praising the beloved at her death; but such a discount would then have to be made of the entire affirmation of Beatrice's miraculous nature in all the other poems, had they too been left to stand alone. In a sense there was nothing new in it. Other poets, like Guido Guinicelli of Bologna and Guido Cavalcanti of Florence, had also written that their ladies were miracles, and we read their praise of them in scattered songs and sonnets. It looks very much like a manner to be granted to lovers who are poets. But they wrote no *Vita Nuova*: nowhere did they surround their poems with a prose which in full seriousness reaffirms all that those poems assert. That is what the prose of the *Vita Nuova* does. And it is prose found written into a Book of Memory. Can such a book be a forgery?

For any such direct and personal concern with Beatrice on

the part of God as here appears in this third *canzone* the reader
is not unprepared. On the contrary, at a point this far along in
the story, he will probably accept it as the most expected of things.
Beatrice, from her first appearance, had worn about her a radiance
which was not that of the natural light of the sun. People seeing
her pass along the street had said: "This is no woman; nay, this is
one of the beautiful angels of Heaven." And we know this, not from
a poet's extravagant rhetoric in rhyme, but from a sober and solemn
and reasoned prose. What others say of Beatrice gives public con-
firmation to what her lover had said of her before, that she seemed
no daughter of man but rather of God. And as for God's personal
concern for her, we had been made ready for that by a stanza in
the first *canzone,* raising the curtain on a little scene in Heaven:

> *Angelo clama in divino intelletto*
> *e dice: "Sire, nel mondo si vede*
> *maraviglia ne l'atto che procede*
> *d'un'anima che'nfin qua sù risplende."*
> *Lo cielo, che non have altro difetto*
> *che d'aver lei, al suo segnor la chiede,*
> *e ciascun santo ne grida merzede.*
> *Sola Pietà nostra parte difende,*
> *che parla Dio, che di madonna intende:*
> *"Diletti miei, or sofferite in pace*
> *che vostra spene sia quanto me piace*
> *là 'v'è alcun che perder lei s'attende,*
> *e che dirà ne lo inferno: O mal nati,*
> *io vidi la speranza de'beati."*

An angel prays in the divine intellect and says: "Lord, in the world
is seen a marvel in the action that proceeds from a soul which shines
even up here." Heaven, which has no other defect than the lack of her,
asks her of its Lord, and every saint cries for this favor. Only Pity takes
our part, for God speaks and his words are of my lady: "Beloved ones,
bear now in peace that, as long as it pleases me, your hope be there
where is one who dreads to lose her and who will say in Hell: O ill-fated
ones, I have seen the hope of those who are in bliss."

Here again (and perhaps especially here, since it is the poet's
declared purpose, beginning with this very *canzone,* to write solely

in praise of his lady), one might take all this to be merely a lover's way of extoling his beloved. But, no. In the *Vita Nuova* there is always the prose to reaffirm the miracle, a prose such as that which describes the effects of Beatrice's greeting and which has in its turn no corresponding poem:

> *Dico che quando ella apparia da parte alcuna, per la speranza de la mirabile salute nullo nemico mi rimanea, anzi mi giugnea una fiamma di caritade, la quale mi facea perdonare a chiunque m'avesse offeso; e chi allora m'avesse domandato di cosa alcuna, la mia risponsione sarebbe stata solamente "Amore," con viso vestito d'umilitade. E quando ella fosse alquanto propinqua al salutare, uno spirito d'amore, distruggendo tutti li altri spiriti sensitivi, pingea fuori li deboletti spiriti del viso, e dicea loro: "Andate a onorare la donna vostra"; ed elli si rimanea nel luogo loro. E chi avesse voluto conoscere Amore, fare lo potea mirando lo tremare de li occhi miei. E quando questa gentilissima salute salutava, non che Amore fosse tal mezzo che potesse obumbrare a me la intollerabile beatitudine, ma elli quasi per soverchio di dolcezza divenia tale, che lo mio corpo, lo quale era tutto allora sotto lo suo reggimento, molte volte si movea come cosa grave inanimata. Sì che appare manifestamente che ne le sue salute abitava la mia beatitudine, la quale molte volte passava e redundava la mia capacitade.*

I say that, whenever she appeared on any side, out of hope for the marvelous greeting I held no one my enemy; nay, a flame of charity overcame me which made me pardon anyone who had offended me; and had anyone asked me then of anything whatsoever, my answer would only have been "love," spoken with face clothed in humility. And when she was about to give her greeting, a spirit of love, destroying all the spirits of the senses, would push out the feeble spirits of sight and say to them "Go honor your mistress"; and he would remain in their place. And whoever might have wished to know Love could have done so by looking at the trembling of my eyes. And when this most gentle lady greeted me, Love was not only no such medium as might shade me from the intolerable beatitude, but he became almost by excess of sweetness such that my body which was then entirely under his rule would move like some heavy inanimate thing. Whereby it plainly appears that in her greetings dwelt my beatitude which many times surpassed and overflowed my capacity.

Here indeed is a power, a "virtue," which can be nothing but supernatural.

It is at her death, however, that the certainty of miracle is strong-
est. For one thing, the mysterious number nine appears again. And
the prose of chapter XXVIII (there is no poem) reports the death of
Beatrice to have been so extraordinary an event that the poet cannot
even write of it. His powers of language are not equal to the task.
To write of her death, moreover, would be to praise himself. Both
are reasons pointing unmistakably to a miracle, to the intervention
of a power above and beyond the natural.

And yet, in spite of these reasons given for not writing of her
death (there is also a third reason which we must consider later),
the author does go on, in a way, to write of it—and not only in a
third *canzone,* as we have seen, but immediately in the prose. He
feels that he must at least say something of that number which has
so often appeared in connection with her life and which is, he sees
now, there at her death: a fact revealed by three different calendars.
According to the Christian way of reckoning time, Beatrice died
in the ninth decade of the thirteenth century of our Lord; according
to the Arabian, she departed this earth in the first hour of the ninth
day of the month; and by the calendar of the Syrians, her death
came in the ninth month of the year. Now one reason why the
number nine was "so friendly to her" might, he says, be this: it
was there to indicate that at her birth all nine of the spheres of
Heaven were in perfect harmony. That would be one reason. But
another more subtle reason might be this: that Beatrice was herself
a number nine—by similitude, that is:

. . . *ma più sottilmente pensando, e secondo la infallible veritade, questo
numero fue ella medesima; per similitudine dico, e ciò intendo così.
Lo numero del tre è la radice del nove, però che, sanza numero altro
alcuno, per se medesimo fa nove, sì come vedemo manifestamente che tre
via tre fa nove. Dunque se lo tre è fattore per se medesimo del nove, e lo
fattore per se medesimo de li miracoli è tre, cioè Padre e Figlio e Spirito
Santo, li quali sono tre e uno, questa donna fue accompagnata da questo
numero del nove a dare ad intendere ch'ella era uno nove, cioè uno
miracolo, la cui radice, cioè del miracolo, è solamente la mirabile Trinitade.*

. . . but thinking more subtly and according to infallible truth, she
was herself this number; I mean by similitude and do so intend. The

number three is the root of nine, since without any other number it makes nine by itself, as we see plainly that three times three makes nine. Therefore, since three is the maker by itself of nine, and the Maker by Itself of miracles is three, that is, Father and Son and Holy Ghost, which are three and one, this lady was accompanied by this number nine in order to signify that she was a nine, that is, a miracle, whose root, that is, of the miracle, is only the marvelous Trinity.

Reason now has discovered what the poet's intuition and the intuition of all who had seen her pass along the way had known already: that Beatrice was a miracle.

*

*   *

Three visions foretell her death. At the time of their coming, no one, not even her lover to whom they came, understood the sad forecast which they so obscurely made. But later, of course, after her death, anyone might see what their true meaning had been. We are told just this of the first of these visions, and it is true of the others as well.

The first vision came as a dream and was made the subject of the first poem in the book. After Beatrice had greeted him the first time, the poet had retired to his room and there a sweet sleep came upon him and in it a marvelous vision. In his room he seemed to see a cloud the color of fire in which he made out the figure of a lord of aspect fearful to behold, seeming exceedingly full of joy and speaking many words, only a few of which the poet could understand; and, among these, the words *Ego dominus tuus.* This lord held in his arms the figure of a lady, nude except for a light wrap of red. Beyond any doubt, this is the figure of the poet's beloved. In his hand the God of Love (nor is there now any doubt either as to the identity of this lord of fearful aspect) is holding something all aflame, of which the poet seems to hear him say: *Vide cor tuum.* Then the God is seen to arouse the lady sleeping in his arms and, with some effort, to make her eat this flaming heart which she does suspiciously. Then Love's joy is changed to bitter tears. He gathers the lady into his arms and with her goes off, weeping, *toward Heaven.*

The poet writes a sonnet on this dream, reporting what he has seen to all the faithful subjects of Love (who are also poets), asking them to reply and to say what its meaning is. Among the answers that came was a poem by Guido Cavalcanti, and this was the beginning of their friendship. But no one, we are told, was able to guess the true meaning of this dream at the time.

It would seem that the faithful subjects of Love were at a considerable disadvantage in this test of their eye for prophecy, since the account of the dream which they received in sonnet form failed to mention the most significant detail of the whole vision, the very sign which made it prophetic and disclosed its true meaning: namely, the detail that Love had gone off with the lady weeping toward Heaven. For only the prose gives this last significant fact, and they saw only the poem.

But it could not have mattered, in any case, for when the author assures us that no one at the time understood the true meaning of this dream, he means to include himself. It is with the vision as it is with the number nine: only *post eventum* can its meaning be seen.

And the number nine is, in fact, connected with this first vision. This much the poet does notice at the time: that it had come to him in the first of the last nine hours of the night. That, too, as he understood later, was in itself a sign pregnant with prophecy.

It is the number nine, indeed, which is the distinguishing mark of all three of the visions foretelling the death of Beatrice. For after the second the poet remembers again to take notice of the time, and he finds that this vision has come in the ninth hour of the day. And again with the third the number is there, for as he then noted, it comes on the ninth day of an illness which had befallen him.

There are other dreams in the *Vita Nuova*. They are rather "daydreams" and are not said to be visions, although a casual reader might take them for such in a quite loose sense of the word. But in the *Vita Nuova* the word vision is not loosely used. At the end of the book we are told how a marvelous vision came to the poet in which he saw things which made him resolve to write no more of Beatrice until he could do so more worthily. No number nine occurs with this vision. But this last is the single exception. Of all the other dreams and daydreams and fantasies which come to the

poet, only three are called visions. The rest are called "imaginations," not visions. The difference is that a vision looks to the
future, as an imagination does not. Moreover, the number nine
occurs only with the first three (genuine) visions. And all three of
these foretell the death of Beatrice. There are in the *Vita Nuova,*
thus, four visions proper. But it seems more significant to see them
as three visions plus one. The underscoring of the number nine
which occurs only with the first three helps to set those off in this
way, making them three against one. In such numbers there is a
special meaning. They, like the number nine, express a mystery.

The true meaning of the second of these three visions marked
by the number nine was, at the time it came, as obscure to the poet
as that of the first. In the second, he makes an especial effort to
understand. He asks to know the meaning of certain obscure words
uttered by the God of Love. But again understanding is denied him.

In its occasion this second vision reminds us, in a way, of the
first. The first had come when he had retired to his room full of
joy at having just been, for the first time, the object of Beatrice's
greeting. Now, on the occasion of the second, that greeting has
just been refused him. As before, he retires to his room, but this
time in order to weep and to lament alone. And there crying mercy
of his lady and calling upon the God of Love for help, he falls
asleep; and the second vision comes to him. In his room, sitting
beside him where he lies, he seems to see a young man clothed in
very white raiment who is looking pensively at him; who, after
some time, seems to call upon the poet, speaking to him these words
in Latin: *Fili mi, tempus est ut pretermictantur simulacra nostra.*
By the first of these words the poet knows that this is his lord, the
God of Love, because he had called him "my son" on other occasions.

Now, as the poet watches, the God breaks into tears and then
seems to expect the poet to speak. So the latter (speaking in the
vernacular, as he always does) makes bold with the question: "Lord
of nobility, why then do you weep?" But once more the God of
Love speaks in Latin, and his answer to the poet's question is this:
*Ego tanquam centrum circuli cui simili modo se habent circum-
ferentie partes; tu autem non sic.*

But what these words can mean as an answer to his question, how it can be that they explain why the God of Love is weeping— this the poet cannot see; and again he says to the figure in white, "What is this, my lord, which you say to me so obscurely?" Whereupon Love shifts to Italian to answer, and curtly replies, "Do not ask to know more than it is useful for you to know."

It is an injunction which the poet apparently obeys. At no point further along in the story does he appear to wonder at the meaning of the obscure words in Latin. And we as readers are obliged for the moment to share in his ignorance. What these words reveal but also withhold, what it is not good that the poet should know at this time, we too must wait to know. Yet it cannot be that in the end we are not supposed to see the meaning of Love's words, any more than it can be that the poet will not later know what they meant. Only if we took the *Vita Nuova* to be a simple record of fact would we expect that to be true. In that case, Love would have spoken just these words in Latin, and the poet would have failed to understand, and that would simply have been that. But we do not take it as such a record. We take it to be a construction informed with the purpose of an author, which purpose is discoverable because it is intentionally revealed when and where the form requires it to be. Love's words are like the number nine and the sign of the true meaning in connection with the first vision: it takes the actual death of Beatrice to make them meaningful as signs and utterances. They are prophetic of her death.

But even when we have seen this to be true, one may still fail to see how it is that Love's obscure words in the second vision speak of the death of Beatrice.

Those words must find their meaning by and in their context. "I am as the center of a circle to which all points of the circumference are equidistant; you are not so." The poet knows Latin, of course. The obscurity is not at all in that; but he is properly baffled by these words because they must be an answer to his own question which asked the God of Love why he began to weep. Love had at first said, "My son, the time has come for us to put aside all our pretenses." By pretenses he must mean such things as the use of screen-ladies to conceal the poet's love for Beatrice.

But why, when Love has said this, should he begin to weep? And how can the words about the center of a circle explain the reason for his tears? The poet may even know that this figure of the circle and the center is one long used to designate the Deity according to His undeniable attribute of transcendental omniscience. And Love is a God and as such may be said to be as the center of a circle in that he is able to see all points on the line of time, past, present, and future, as if they were points on the circumference of a circle and hence all equidistant from him. Which would mean that the God of Love is saying that he is a God and that the poet is not (*tu autem non sic*). But that is precisely why, as a reply to the poet's question, those words seem wholly obscure. For the poet most surely knows that Love is a God and that he himself is not. And since this had been true all along, how can this be a reason for tears at this time? What the poet does not see is that by the figure of the circle and the center of a circle the God of Love has told him, not so much that he is a God and that the poet is not, as that, being a God, he, unlike the poet, can see into the future. It is the fact that he knows the future which explains why the God begins to weep when he has said that the time has come when they must put aside their pretenses. The time has come because the God can see what will now not long delay in coming to pass: the death of Beatrice. Her death, he can see, is imminent. That is why it is time to renounce their game of concealment. As it is, the poet will know only too soon that Beatrice will die. That is why he is not helped to understand the prophecy of her death here, and is enjoined not to ask to know what it would do him no good to know.

The shift from Latin to the vernacular on the part of the God of Love when he utters these last words is in itself a part of the total revelation made by the vision. For only the words in Latin are of the nature of oracle, and by being put in that language they are set apart and raised to a proper dignity. When Love changes to Italian one feels that somehow he has stepped down to the level of the poet and of everyday affairs. Thus, like the number nine, the Latin too is a sign.

*

*   *

As for the third vision of the *Vita Nuova,* it is not without reason that the name of vision is withheld from it when the account of it is given. And yet the reason for this is one which we shall not see unless we realize how it is that the particular requirements of the unfolding of a revelation as it is done in this story are met in this way. To deny to this vision the name of vision at the time it is narrated is simply to keep to the point of view of the protagonist who cannot yet know that it is a true vision. This is a protagonist upon whom the death of Beatrice is to break with the shock of a thing in no way expected. To call this vision a vision would be to point out its prophetic nature. Now the name, to be sure, had been given to those first two dreams which brought omens of the approaching event. But, with these first two, there was no real danger that they would give away their secret. For one thing, the death of Beatrice was no actual part of what they displayed. But with the third vision we are on the verge of the event itself. Moreover, unlike the other two, this third gives us not a mere sign of Beatrice's death, but the very event itself. In this third vision, the death of Beatrice is actually experienced. To call it a vision would be to give away the secret so jealously kept up to now. If her real death, which is now not far off, is to come with any surprise, it is important that what is seen be seen for the moment from the point of view of an unsuspecting protagonist. A post of observation in ignorance and wonderment must be strictly kept, especially at this point. Later he will see that what he took to be a mere delirium was a vision like the other two visions foretelling the death of Beatrice.

The third is that vision which we observed at the outset to occupy the center of the *Vita Nuova* (chapter xxiii) and to be replete with meaning for the whole construction. That it comes on the ninth day of an illness suffered by the poet is a telling sign. His pain on that day had greatly increased and had caused him to think on his own frail life. And this thought in turn had brought him to reflect that one day the most gentle Beatrice must surely die. Whereupon a swoon came upon him, and he closed his eyes and entered into what seemed a kind of delirium. In the narrating of it, a noticeable stress is put on the fact that what he now sees can be no more than the result of an imagination which is sick, no more than the raving of a feverish mind. Faces of disheveled women appear before him saying: "You will die." After these come others horrible to see, who speak to him saying: "You are dead." The fantasy grows so wild that he no longer knows where he is. Again he sees women with hair in disarray, going about weeping and wondrously sad. The sun grows dark and the stars come out with a color as if they were weeping. Birds fall dead from the air, and there are great earthquakes. Then a friend appears before him saying: "Don't you know? Your marvelous lady has departed this earth." He looks then toward Heaven and seems to see a multitude of angels returning upward, having before them a little cloud which is very white; they are heard to sing gloriously, and *Hosanna in excelsis* is their song. Then the sick man's heart tells him that his lady must be dead. And his feverish fantasy even wanders so from real things that it shows him Beatrice lying dead. Women are covering her head with a white veil, and her face expresses so much humility that it seems to say, "I am where I see the source of all peace." Then her lover calls upon Death to come and to take him too, for already he can see that his own face wears the pallor of death. In his delirium he calls out and has already uttered the name of Beatrice when a lady sitting by to watch over him arouses him.

Such is the third and last of the visions forecasting the imminent death of Beatrice.

Because of what this vision has witnessed, Beatrice may be said to die twice in the *Vita Nuova:* once in the illusory space of what is called a delirium, and then really. But the reader will remark that, further along, when she really dies, her death is hardly spoken of as a death at all. It is rather "a departure from us." Having the context that it has, is this not something more than the familiar euphemism for death? Somehow, when Beatrice really dies, her death seems less like a death than it does an ascension. Her lover will not write of it, he says, for reasons which point clearly to a miraculous event. Over the real event when it comes, a curtain is dropped. Of her real death we are given no particulars. And yet the reader will note that he does not feel cheated. Nor is he inclined to be incredulous at the suggestion of miracle. For already in the third vision he has been present, as it were, at the death of Beatrice, even though all the while that he witnessed it, its reality was denied.

But such a denial cannot cancel the vividness of the impressions the experience in vision has left with him. To the real death of Beatrice, which he is not permitted to witness, the reader comes bringing details remembered from a visionary death. In short, he does what the author of the *Vita Nuova* was artist enough to know he would do.

*

*   *

But the death of Beatrice in a vision is more than the sign of her real death to come. It is the revelation of a resemblance so striking that few readers, at least few Christian readers, can fail to take notice of it. Those very portents which come with her death— the earthquake, the darkening of the sun—how may these not call to mind the death of another, the death of Christ? In the account in the *Vita Nuova* there are to be sure certain details which are not in the Gospels: birds fall from the air and the stars that come out in the ominous dusk appear to weep; women with hair torn in grief go about and are wondrously sad. But these are no more than details which one easily imagines some Italian painter adding to his canvas of the Crucifixion. They are all indubitable signs of universal cataclysm such as had only been seen when Christ had died. So strong indeed is the suggestion of the resemblance in this respect that one might be shocked at the audacity of it, if he did not remember that, in the case of Beatrice, no real reality is attributed to these things. They are seen in a kind of nightmare which came as the result of an illness, and as such we accept them without protesting.

Were any reader reluctant to see in Beatrice that resemblance to Christ which this vision of her death had indicated, then it would appear as if the author of the *Vita Nuova* had anticipated his particular recalcitrance here; since, in the chapter immediately following this vision, he has brought out her resemblance to Christ

with so striking an emphasis that all readers must yield before it
and know without further doubt that the comparison is in accord
with the conscious intention of the author.

For, on a day following this third vision, the poet had had
another of his so-called "imaginations": he knew by a certain quak-
ing in his heart that the marvelous Beatrice must be approaching.
Such joy filled his heart that it seemed not *his* heart at all, and the
God of Love came to his heart and took up his place there. Then
the poet saw coming toward him a lady famous for her beauty and
once the beloved of his first friend, Cavalcanti. The lady's name
was Giovanna, but because of her beauty she was also called *Primavera* (Spring). And following her came the wondrous Beatrice:

*. . . io vidi venire verso me una gentile donna, la quale era di famosa
bieltade, e fue già molto donna di questo primo mio amico. E lo nome
di questa donna era Giovanna, salvo che per la sua bieltade, secondo che
altri crede, imposto l'era nome Primavera; e così era chiamata. E appresso lei, guardando, vidi venire la mirabile Beatrice. Queste donne
andaro presso di me così l'una appresso l'altra, e parve che Amore mi
parlasse nel cuore e dicesse: "Quella prima è nominata Primavera solo
per questa venuta d'oggi; chè io mossi lo imponitore del nome a chia-
marla così Primavera, cioè prima verrà lo die che Beatrice si mosterrà
dopo la imaginazione del suo fedele. E se anche vogli considerare lo
primo nome suo, tanto è quanto dire 'prima verrà,' però che lo suo nome
Giovanna è da quello Giovanni lo quale precedette la verace luce,
dicendo:* Ego vox clamantis in deserto: parate viam Domini" [chapter
xxiv].

. . . I saw coming toward me a gentle lady who was famous for her
beauty and who had once been the beloved of my first friend. And the
name of this lady was Joan, except that because of her beauty, as some
believe, she had been given the name of Primavera and so she was called.
And after her, as I looked, I saw the marvelous Beatrice coming. These
ladies passed by me thus one after the other and it seemed to me that
Love spoke in my heart and said: "She who comes first is named Primavera, solely because of this coming today; because I moved the giver of
the name to call her Primavera, that is, *prima verrà* [she-will-come-first]
on the day that Beatrice will show herself following the imagination of
her faithful servant. And if you will consider her original name, it is
the same as saying *prima verrà* since her name Joan is from that John

who preceded the true light, saying: *Ego vox clamantis in deserto: parate viam Domini."*

For the reader of the *Vita Nuova* who is seeking to grasp the principle of its unity and the secret of its form, a new light dawns with these words spoken by Love. What had been before only scattered detail now shows a certain magnetic attraction towards a single idea, and toward what is perhaps the controlling metaphor of the whole construction: a certain resemblance of Beatrice to Christ. He will see from this most explicit declaration of that resemblance, moreover, one thing of the greatest importance for the understanding of the whole work: that is, the nature itself of this resemblance. It is a resemblance of analogy. This is not allegory. Where one has read *Beatrice* in the story up to now, or in the story as it continues, one may not now substitute *Christ.* Beatrice is *as* Christ, and because this is true, the lady who comes before her is as John the Baptist. But this analogy is a matter which, because of its importance, demands a detailed and more considered examination than may be afforded at this point. For the moment let us enjoy the light cast over the whole story by this resemblance made now so boldly explicit, and know that we had had intimations of it before. That figure dressed in white raiment whom the poet had seen sitting beside his bed (because of the fact which we now know, that he brought with him the message and imminent sense of the death of Beatrice) now reminds us of that angel dressed all in white who was found sitting at the tomb of our Saviour. Even the choice of certain words in speaking of Beatrice, moreover, to one sensitive to overtones, seems now pregnant with the concealed metaphor; especially if one knows that the Old Testament, through the voice of its prophets and the Psalmist, had many times spoken of Christ as our *salus.* It is a usage which Dante echoed in his treatise on monarchy (written in Latin) when he spoke of Christ with the phrase *salus noster salutabat.* In the *Vita Nuova,* as early as chapter xi, of Beatrice it is said, *quando questa gentilissima salute salutava.* May we see this as anything but another glimmer of that basic metaphor which, thanks to the words of Love in chapter xxiv, is now openly declared?

The whole light from it falls on yet other parts of the work. Now one sees by it an even deeper reason why a "second" death of Beatrice resembles an ascension more than it does a death. And we may be almost startled, moreover, suddenly to see a better reason why a number nine should be connected with Beatrice and especially with her death and the visions of her death, remembering that it was in the ninth hour that Christ gave up the ghost. And this same resemblance to Christ—is it not to be found in all parts of this story, uplifting, for instance, and expanding the grief of her lover, when she has left him alone on this earth, to a kind of universal sadness and a sense of loss to the whole world? The underground presence, as it were, of that resemblance makes the words of Jeremiah, *Quomodo sedet sola civitas plena populo! facta est quasi vidua domina gentium,* not too lofty and sacred a proclamation of the death of a mortal creature. Does not that same hidden metaphor explain why the poet addresses the "princes of the earth" when he proclaims her death? And explain, too, how it is not unfitting that pilgrims on their way to Rome to behold the Veronica, the image of the departed Christ, should be told of the grief of a city which a departed *beatrice* has left desolate like an earthly Jerusalem which has lost its saviour?

We see now many things with a new understanding, among them a most striking reason for the kind of predictions which had come revealing and yet withholding the truth that Beatrice was to die. It is natural, we now see, that these should be like those utterances in the Gospels which foretell the death and resurrection of the Son of Man and yet conceal this from his disciples. The eyes of the disciples were opened *after* His death. But at the time when these things were spoken we read:

Let these sayings sink down into your ears: for the Son of Man shall be delivered into the hands of men.

But they understood not this saying, and it was hid from them, that they perceived it not; and they feared to ask him of that saying.

With Beatrice's lover it was not otherwise when by three different visions he was told of her death that was to come. Their true meaning was hid from him at the time. But his eyes, like the eyes of the disciples, were opened later by the event itself.

Then afterwards, reading in the book of his memory, he also could see that the death of his lady stood at the center of his New Life. And we in our turn, as readers of this copy from the book of his memory, may see that the poet's new life in love is very much like a little world reflecting the larger one. For even as (in the medieval view) the death of our Lord Jesus Christ stands at the center of the whole Christian universe, saying what *now* is and what *then* is; and even as all things that come before His death look forward to it and all things that come after His death look back upon it: just so is the death of Beatrice in that litttle world of the *Vita Nuova* where Beatrice is, as Christ is in the real world whose author is God.

II

The Book of Memory

WITH the death of Beatrice, a circle is closed. We know again what we began by knowing. And we stand at a point where we can see that the movement along the line of this action is not movement in a single direction. The current is alternating, which is something one had already seen in the figure of a poet-protagonist become two persons according to a situation in time: the one being he who, though ignorant of the end, moves always toward the end; and the other he who, knowing the end, is constantly retracing the whole line of events with the new awareness and transcendent understanding which such superior knowledge can give.

There is an image at the very beginning of the *Vita Nuova* which serves to cast the whole outline of its form into just these terms, a metaphor which is as the door to the action beyond. Without passing through it we cannot enter into the little world of miracle of the *Vita Nuova*. And when we do pass through, certain conditions are thrust upon us which we have no choice but to accept. The nature of what lies beyond, in a sense the very way in which things on the inside are to be seen, is established here. Nor does the author intend that we should forget this, once we are inside.

In giving his first reason for not writing of Beatrice's death (chapter XXVIII), for instance, he seems to have taken us by the hand, to have led us back to that entranceway and said, "Look: remember the way you came in here, remember on what conditions." The first of the three reasons he gives is this:

E avvegna che forse piacerebbe a presente trattare alquanto de la sua partita da noi, non è lo mio intendimento di trattarne qui per tre ragioni: la prima è che ciò non è del presente proposito, se volemo guardare nel proemio che precede questo libello.

And although it might be pleasing were I now to treat somewhat of her departure from us, it is not my intention to treat of that here

25

109170

for three reasons: the first is that that is no part of the present purpose, if we will consider the proem which precedes this little book.

Even the most attentive reader of the *Vita Nuova* may have been unaware up to this point that the book had any such thing as a proem. As such, it will not be indicated in any edition that he may have of the work. However, "the proem which precedes this little book" cannot be other than what in all editions is printed as the first chapter of the work, a chapter only two sentences long:

> *In quella parte del libro della mia memoria dinanzi a la quale poco si potrebbe leggere, si trova una rubrica la quale dice:* INCIPIT VITA NOVA. *Sotto la quale rubrica io trovo scritte le parole le quali è mio intendimento d'assemplare in questo libello: e se non tutte, almeno la loro sentenzia.*

In that part of the book of my memory before which little could be read is found a rubric which says: INCIPIT VITA NOVA [Here beginneth the New Life]. Under which rubric I find written the words which it is my intention to copy into this little book; and if not all, at least their substance.

This is the whole of the Proem to the *Vita Nuova,* and this is the opening metaphor of the book. In the end it proves to be much more than just a pretty way of saying what might have been said in a more straightforward fashion. It could, of course, have been ornamental and still have served a sufficient purpose. It might, that is, have been an author's way of saying with some color of rhetoric that he had resolved to write this little book about a certain part of his past and that this was to be a faithful report of what he could remember of it. In this sense the metaphor might have been used for what it was worth at the moment and then have been dropped. But the *Vita Nuova* is not built like that. As the book develops, we know that this first image has not been abandoned, and we are reminded of this as early as the end of the second chapter, where we read:

> *E però che soprastare a le passioni e atti di tanta gioventudine pare alcuno parlare fabuloso, mi partirò da esse; e trapassando molte cose le quali si potrebbero trarre de l'essemplo onde nascono queste, verrò a*

quelle parole le quali sono scritte ne la mia memoria sotto maggiori paragrafi.

And since to dwell on the passions and actions of such early youth seems something of a fabulous tale, I will leave them; and passing over many things which might be taken from the original whence these come, I will come to those words which are written in my memory under larger paragraphs.

Here the metaphor of the Proem still holds. It may not be strictly kept at all times in the course of this story. Some few times it will appear to suffer total eclipse. Neither is there any danger that it may be taken literally, that it may be seen, that is, as no metaphor at all. But, in any event, already at this early point in the story the reader is obliged to notice that the form (in one sense) of the book is growing out of the image in the Proem and harking back to that image as it grows.

Is this true for the whole of the *Vita Nuova?*

It is. And to see how this is true, to observe how by this image the whole work is cast into a mold which constitutes the first outline of its form is, one discovers, a delight to the mind. And since, as far along as chapter xxviii and the actual death of Beatrice, the reader is still referred back to this figure of a book at the beginning, it is important that we see from the outset what its implications are.

Let us first realize that this Book of Memory is no modern book. The words in it are written, not printed. It is a *liber scriptus* of the thirteenth century, and it is being published as books were published in that century, patiently, with pen and ink, one copy at a time. Publication is the work of a scribe, whose business it is to make copies of books.

A matter, no doubt, sufficiently plain to most readers. But however obvious, it is not to be excluded from our awareness as we read. A reader whose eye is accustomed to printed books must see that the Proem of the *Vita Nuova* does not hold up the picture of a man engaged in the extraordinary act of copying a book by hand. On the contrary, it is the picture of a quite usual enterprise. Here is simply a scribe at his proper task. Before him he has his text (*assemplo*) and it is his job to reproduce that text (*assemplare*), letter by letter and page by page faithfully.

Thus, to take the image somewhat strictly, it would appear that we have no right to see an author in the scene presented by it. All we are given to see is a manuscript book open at a rubric (no doubt set off boldly in red) which reads INCIPIT VITA NOVA, and a scribe who is just beginning to make a copy of what he finds already written down there under that rubric.

But in any event it is evident, too, that this scribe claims for himself the privilege of a greater liberty with the original text than any ordinary copyist would have any right to. The Proem is his statement of what he will do as scribe. At the end of its second sentence he says that if he does not copy down all of the words of his text, he will at least give their *sentenzia,* that is, the substance of what they say. And the license which this scribe is taking evidently lies in this: that he may choose or not to copy down all the words of the original before him. Indeed, one has already witnessed an instance of this at the end of chapter II, where the scribe decided to skip to more important paragraphs in the Book of Memory.

To be sure, it is because this is the book of his own memory that he has any right to do such a thing. Even so, this is a considerable liberty for any scribe to be taking. Such a privilege as this, claimed at the very outset, is in fact a kind of charter giving to this copyist the right to decide what to abridge of the original text. The gravity of such a privilege is heightened, moreover, by our realization that no one other than this scribe can ever have access to the original of this book. All that we shall ever see of that original is the copy which he will now make for us, and we must submit to his will almost as to that of an author.

This is the Book of *his* Memory. And the further fact that it contains poems of which he is the author brings yet another unusual feature into the picture. With the sonnet of chapter III, the first in the book, we meet in this scribe a poet. This is his poem. As he copies, he is rewriting words which he himself first wrote down. He is, thus, author at least of some of the words in the original before him, and for that reason would seem to have all the more right to select and abridge. Hence, in chapter IV of the copy he gives us, no poem is copied down out of the Book of Memory although the reader is told that on the occasion described in that chapter a poem was written. This scribe, therefore, is not even giving all of that part of the original text of which he himself is the author.

With such a literal interpretation of this image of a book one may be inclined to lose patience. Nevertheless, he will discover that he is obliged at more than one point in the story to accept it in just such literal terms.

One of these points is chapter xxv. Here, too, is a place far along in the book where conditions fixed by the Proem are seen still to obtain.

In chapter xxv, the poet shows concern to justify something that he had done in the preceding poem. There he had written of Love as if Love were a person, someone who could talk and walk and laugh. But, he argues now in the prose, poets have after all a right to do such things as this, even if they are not according to the truth. In the course of his argument one finds the following:

Onde, con ciò sia cosa che a li poete sia conceduta maggiore licenza di parlare che a li prosaici dittatori, e questi dicitori per rima non siano altro che poete volgari, degno e ragionevole è che a loro sia maggiore licenzia largita di parlare che a li altri parlatori volgari.

Wherefore, inasmuch as a greater license of speech is granted to the poets [ancient poets] than to writers in prose, and these writers in rhyme are none other than poets in the vernacular, it is right that to them a greater license of expression should be granted than to other writers in the vernacular.

The point of interest to us for the moment is incidental in this argument but is unmistakably clear. It is that the personification of Love (and hence, in general, any personification) is not something which writers of prose may indulge in. About this there seems to be no doubt at all in the poet's mind. His argument appeals to it, in fact, as to the firmest kind of assumption.

But if it is true that writers of prose may not use personifications, then the reader will hardly avoid certain reflections of his own on what he has so far met with in this very book. He is not likely to forget instances to be found, not in the poems, but only in the prose, where Love has appeared as a person who could not only talk and walk and laugh, but could weep and make oracular utterances in Latin. He will recall, for instance, quite clearly that second vision which had come in this story a good way back of this point (chapter xii), where the personification of Love is indeed mainly a thing of the prose. Love comes there as a young man dressed in white, and little of what he is seen to do in the prose narrative becomes a part of the poem that is given. How then can the poet turn his back on what has been done in prose in the preceding chapters of his own book? How can he honestly do this?

Obviously, the answer to these questions is to be found only in the Proem. And by such reflections as these the reader is again brought back sharply to the image there and reminded that the conditions established by it still obtain, even in chapter xxv.

That answer is simply that the author of the poems of the *Vita Nuova* is not the author of its prose; at least, not of a considerable part of its prose. And how this must be so is plain on rereading the Proem. But precisely in doing this we should note that, without that Proem and the particular picture presented by it, such an argument as this about what poets may do and what writers of prose may not do would be completely confusing. And that, however obvious, is for the moment the point of importance.

It has not proved to be so obvious, one may note in passing, either to those scholars who have seen allegory everywhere in the *Vita Nuova,* or to their opponents in a long polemic who everywhere have seen facts and real events. It is typical of these two embattled schools of what passes for criticism that neither the one nor the other has ever been willing to submit to the rule of the image which we have been following and to accept the fact that, once we have passed beyond the Proem, that image is as the law of the place into which we have entered. We become its subjects. And, on the inside, the realist may not ask his questions of reality nor his opponent his questions of allegory unless this is permitted (and often enough it is not) by the terms of that initial metaphor which governs the whole.

To forget those terms is to be completely baffled by the first reason given in chapter xxviii for not writing of Beatrice's death. Let us see that reason again:

E avvegna che forse piacerebbe a presente trattare alquanto de la sua partita da noi, non è lo mio intendimento di trattarne qui per tre ragioni: la prima è che ciò non è del presente proposito, se volemo guardare nel proemio che precede questo libello.

And although it might be pleasing were I now to treat somewhat of her departure from us, it is not my intention to treat of that here for three reasons: the first is that that is no part of the present purpose, if we will consider the proem which precedes this little book.

But how now is this? How can the Proem give such an obvious reason for not writing of Beatrice's death? And what does it mean that the reader should now be asked to turn back to the beginning to discover such a reason?

It means this: that by looking back to the Proem, the reader will be reminded of that situation in time which the picture presented there serves to establish throughout the whole *Vita Nuova*. A scribe has engaged to copy words which he finds already written down under a certain rubric in a book open before him. His first job— the only job which he has undertaken at all, according to the Proem—is to copy. Thus, a first reason given for not writing of Beatrice's death need be only a reminder to the reader that it was never the declared intention of this scribe to write (*trattare*) himself of anything; and that to do so now, to compose any account whatever *now,* would not be according to his statement of intention as scribe in the Proem.

Here is a point in Dante studies where one has learned to expect the "realist" to enter with heavy step, demanding to know what all this really means. He has little time to waste with fancy; he is after the truth and the facts are the truth. Has not Dante promised to report these things according to his recollection of them? Was there then nothing in his memory concerning the actual death of Beatrice? Does this mean that Dante was unable to remember anything at all about her death? And if so, then why? Was he perhaps so overcome by the shock of it that his mind went blank at the time; and hence, later, he simply had no memory of the event to report?

The temptation to regard this book as a biographical document will no doubt prove always too much for many of its readers, and we shall have to learn a certain resignation before such questions which will surely continue to be addressed to this text. Meanwhile, however, what would seem fairly obvious may only be patiently pointed out: that to yield to such temptation means to attempt to rewrite the *Vita Nuova,* for only by rewriting it could we force it to make an answer to such questions as these. For the book as it stands is not in the least concerned with answering them and makes no reply at all. And one may always prefer to take it as it stands.

But one thing is evident: this scribe who is also the author of the poems seems to remember very well the circumstances and the details of her death. If he did not, he might not advance his other two reasons for not writing of that event: first, that he cannot find words equal to the task of reporting it; and second, that, even if he could, to do so would be to write in praise of himself. Both are reasons which make it quite clear that his memory has not failed him. Moreover, in a third *canzone* written later, he has told something of the death of Beatrice, declaring it, as we have seen, to be a miracle.

His first reason, then, is simply that it is not according to his intention as stated in the Proem to be anything but a scribe. To write here and now of anything at all is simply not according to that intention; and it is one which he expects his reader to respect.

And yet, at the very moment when he insists so strictly that his role now is only that of scribe, he chooses to depart from that role. For, he goes on to say, there is one matter that ought after all to be dealt with. So that, having given his three reasons, he continues:

Tuttavia, però che molte volte lo numero del nove ha preso luogo tra le parole dinanzi, onde pare che sia non sanza ragione, e ne la sua partita cotale numero pare che avesse molto luogo, convenesi di dire quindi alcuna cosa, acciò che pare al proposito convenirsi. Onde prima dicerò come ebbe luogo ne la sua partita e poi n'assegnerò alcuna ragione per che questo numero fue a lei cotanto amico.

And yet, since many times the number nine has occurred among the words up to now, wherefore it would seem to be not without some reason; and in her departure it seems to have had a large place; it is fitting that something should be said of this, since it seems to be relevant to our purpose. Wherefore first I will tell how it had a part in her departure and then I will give some reason why this number was so friendly to her.

There was something peculiar to be noted in the words of the book he had been copying—something which again with the death of Beatrice was to be seen: a number nine. And so much does the peculiar way in which that number has occurred call for some special comment at this point that this scribe does after all go beyond the limits of being merely a scribe. He writes forthwith a brief treatise on the meaning of this number; a treatise which, one may observe, is as much beside his original intention as any account of the death of Beatrice would have been had he written that now and inserted it here instead. Still, there is this matter of a number so striking in the way it has occurred all the while in connection with Beatrice that something ought to be said of it. And he writes accordingly a chapter assigning some reasons for the frequent occurrence of that number.

It is encouraging to this interpretation of a much-debated passage to note that the scribe had indulged in this sort of "digression" before. Toward the end of chapter x he had copied from the Book of Memory the following words:

. . . passando per alcuna parte, mi negò lo suo dolcissimo salutare ne lo quale stava tutta la mia beatitudine.

. . . and passing by a certain place she denied me her sweet greeting in which dwelt all my beatitude.

Then, to introduce his next chapter, he concluded as follows:

E uscendo alquanto del proposito presente, voglio dare ad intendere quello che lo suo salutare in me vertuosamente operava.

And departing somewhat from the present purpose, I wish to set forth what effects the virtue of her greeting produced in me.

Whereupon the chapter, so introduced, goes on to become a little treatise on the effects of Beatrice's greeting. And when he has finished what is, as he says, "somewhat beside his intention," this scribe goes back to his copying and to his following chapter with the remark,

Ora tornando al proposito . . .

Now, to come back to the subject . . .

Why was it a digression from "the subject" to describe the effects of Beatrice's greeting when anything at all connected with Beatrice would seem to be of the essence of his subject? Because this chapter xi is a chapter written *now* by the scribe, written now and in the present tense, as the reader will note, and hence not according to the intention declared in the Proem.

Chapter xxix on the number nine is just such a digression, too.

*

*   *

In order to do this, in order to write in the present tense in this way, this scribe (who was given to us as scribe by the image of the Proem) has had to become what he himself has supplied a name for in concluding his reasons for not writing of Beatrice's death. That, he says, he will leave to some other *chiosatore*. But this scribe becomes himself just such a person as that word names when, in spite of reasons given for not doing so, he proceeds to write a little treatise on the number nine. Then he is no longer a scribe. He is now a *chiosatore* himself.

The words "glosser" and "glossator" are obsolete in English. "Gloss" in the sense of "commentary" is more familiar to us. A *chiosatore* is the writer of a gloss. And a gloss is precisely what this chapter xxix on the number nine is.

When we shall have conducted our analysis far enough to see how this is, the total implications of the image of a Book in the Proem will have revealed themselves to be involved and somewhat complex. But they need not, for all that, be confusing. Briefly, the situation is this: some parts of this Book of Memory were written in the past and some are being written now. The poems belong to the past. And that prose which stands around the poems in the original Book of Memory also belongs to the past. But let us remember that not all of the prose in the copy we have was found in the original. For here and there the scribe has added to that original text, and his additions are glosses. They are conceived in the present tense.

Of course, we know that the *prose* which the poet finds already inscribed in the original, and which is therefore in the past tense, is not his. For that prose actually is prose only through metaphor. The "words" which compose it are words only by virtue of a figure which gives them such metaphorical meaning. They are in reality not words at all but real things and events.

A strictly literal analysis of an image and its implications may be excused, perhaps, if it has brought us to see that the original of this Book of Memory (what the scribe first finds to copy from) is made up both of words which were, first of all, (and outside of any metaphor) words: and of yet other words which out of metaphor are not words at all. The first are, of course, those words which are the poems. The second are those "words" in prose which the poet, having resolved to become the scribe of the Book of his Memory, finds surrounding his poems. These "words," unlike the words of the poems, are not his. That is why, when he denies the license of personification to writers of prose, he does not have to take into account any such "writing" as this. For if this is prose, it is "prose," after all, of a quite special sort.

And it is also because the words of this "prose" are words which he did not himself write that the scribe is now justified in turning back over them and discovering a hidden meaning in them. As he does this we observe that he respects the metaphor of the Proem, in virtue of which he writes now on a number nine not as the *event* which it is out of metaphor, but on a number nine as a word among words, a word which, as he says, "has taken place among the preceding words." The way in which this turn of phrase keeps the terms of the metaphor in the Proem is impressive. It further emphasizes the fact that those prose words among which this scribe finds this number nine are none of his doing. The number nine in that phrase is the subject of the verb: *it* has taken place among the preceding words. We remember now that the Proem has said that these words were *found* in the Book of his Memory. They have an objective existence there. They can be read and copied. The scribe can survey them as he copies and observe that among them this number nine is to be seen here and here and here again. There must then be some special meaning in this. And the reader, by the copy he has, can see in his turn what the scribe himself had found in the original, namely, that the first word of the text before him was "nine": *"Nove* fiate già." Nine is the first word of the *Vita Nuova* proper. That it should occupy that special place, and the several other special places which it has there, cannot be without significance.

We shall do well to have now the whole argument of chapter xxix before us. To many readers of the *Vita Nuova* in modern times, it has inevitably seemed strangely fantastic and "medieval"; and, on the part of some of those Dante scholars who have paid particular attention to it, one detects, I believe, a feeling which betrays a slight touch of shame: shame that the Master should ever have indulged in this sort of superstitious nonsense. For this is the gloss he wrote on the death of Beatrice:

Io dico che, secondo l'usanza d'Arabia, l'anima sua nobilissima si partio ne la prima ora del nono giorno del mese; e secondo l'usanza di Siria, ella si partio nel nono mese de l'anno, però che lo primo mese è ivi Tisirin primo, lo quale a noi è Ottobre; e secondo l'usanza nostra, ella si partio in quello anno de la nostra indizione, cioè de li anni Domini, in cui lo perfetto numero nove volte era compiuto in quello centinaio nel quale in questo mondo ella fue posta, ed ella fue de li cristani del terzodecimo centinaio. Perchè questo numero fosse in tanto amico di lei, questa potrebbe essere una ragione: con ciò sia cosa che, secondo Tolomeo e secondo la cristiana veritate, nove siano li cieli che si muovono, e, secondo comune oppinione astrologa, li detti cieli adoperino qua giuso secondo la loro abitudine insieme, questo numero fue amico di lei per dare ad intendere che ne la sua generazione tutti e nove i mobili cieli perfettissimamente s'aveano insieme. Questa è una ragione di ciò; ma più sottilmente pensando, e secondo la infallibile veritade, questo numero fue ella medesima; per similitudine dico, e ciò intendo così. Lo numero del tre è la radice del nove, però che, sanza numero altro alcuno, per se medesimo fa nove, sì come vedemo manifestamente che tre via tre fa nove. Dunque se lo tre è fattore per se medesimo del nove e lo fattore per se medesimo de li miracoli è tre, cioè Padre e Figlio e Spirito Santo, li quali sono tre e uno, questa donna fue accompagnata da questo numero del nove a dare ad intendere ch'ella era uno nove, cioè uno miracolo, la cui radice, cioè del miracolo, è solamente la mirabile Trinitade. Forse ancora per più sottile persona si

*vederebbe in ciò più sottile ragione; ma questa è quella ch'io ne veggio,
e che più mi piace.*

I say that, according to the Arabian calendar, her very noble soul
departed in the first hour of the ninth day of the month; and according
to the Syrian calendar, it departed in the ninth month of the year, because the first month there is Tixryn I, which is October with us; and
by our own calendar it departed in that year of our indiction, that is,
of the years of our Lord, in which the perfect number [ten] was completed for the ninth time in that century in which she was brought into
this world, and she was among the Christians of the thirteenth century.
One reason why this number was friendly to her could be this: inasmuch
as, according to Ptolemy and according to Christian truth, nine are the
heavens that move, and according to common astrological opinion, the
said heavens work their effects down here according to their inter-
relations, this number was friendly to her in order to show that at her
generation all nine of the mobile heavens were in perfect relation one
to another.   This is one reason thereof; but thinking more subtly and
according to infallible truth, she was herself this number; I mean by
similitude and do so intend.   The number three is the root of nine,
since without any other number it makes nine by itself, as we see plainly
that three times three makes nine.   Therefore, since three is the maker
by itself of nine and the maker by itself of miracles is three, that is,
Father and Son and Holy Ghost, which are three and one, this lady was
accompanied by this number nine in order to signify that she was a
nine, that is, a miracle, whose root, that is, of the miracle, is only the
marvelous Trinity.   Perhaps a more subtle person would see in that a more
subtle reason; but this is the one which I see in it and which I like best.

This gloss and all the other products of that metaphor of a Book
of Memory which converts things and events to so many *words*
will seem quaint to a modern reader of the *Vita Nuova,* and (what
is even more unfortunate) perhaps wholly arbitrary.   But to a
reader of Dante's time they would have been neither.   To him there
was little if anything new in this metaphor, and certainly nothing
at all new in the way of looking at the world which it implied.
For to the reader of that century, already and without any metaphor
of a "book of memory," it was possible, even reasonable, to regard
the things and events of our real world as so many words in a
book, the Book of the Created Universe.   Indeed, that more general

metaphor of such a book was already to him so acceptable that to this reader it might well seem that it was not so much the particular image of a Book of Memory which made it possible to view things as words, as it was that other and more generally recognized image of a Book of the Universe. At any rate (and this is rather what matters) this metaphor of the Book of Memory, at the time it was used in the *Vita Nuova,* was under no strain of novelty or arbitrariness, and did no great violence to real things and events in making them into words.

Science has long since abandoned any view of nature making possible such a metaphor as that of a Book of the Universe, since that figure clearly implies an "author" (whom modern science cannot afford to contemplate within its own method) and assumes an original creation (which our science is most unwilling to talk about). But to any scientist as late as the seventeenth century, that metaphor and the conception of the world which it expressed were still familiar. Galileo was able to make an interesting use of the figure. It adorns the prose of Browne's *Religio Medici.* This way of viewing the world as a creation having an author belongs primarily to the Christian and Judeo-Christian tradition. But we do not need to inquire here into its origin. Enough if we know, for purposes of reading the *Vita Nuova,* that the figure had wide currency before and in Dante's time. Hugh of St. Victor (1096-1141), a mystic who is allotted a lofty place in the *Paradiso,* puts it, for instance, this way:

> *Universus enim mundus iste sensibilis quasi quidam liber est scriptus digito Dei, hoc est virtute divina creatus, et singulae creaturae quasi figurae quaedam sunt non humano placito inventae sed divino arbitrio institutae ad manifestandam invisibilium Dei sapientiam. Quemadmodum autem si illiteratus quis apertum librum videat, figuras aspicit, litteras non cognoscit: ita stultus et animalis homo qui non percipit ea quae Dei sunt (I Cor. II) in visibilibus istis creaturis foris videt speciem sed intus non intelligit rationem. Qui autem spiritualis est ed omnia dijudicare potest, in eo quidem quod foris considerat pulchritudinem operis, intus concipit quam miranda sit sapientia Creatoris.*

For this whole visible world is as a book written by the finger of God, that is, created by divine power, and individual creatures are as figures not devised by human will but instituted by divine authority to show forth the wisdom of the invisible things of God. But just as some illiterate man who sees an open book, looks at the figures, but does not recognize the letters: just so the foolish and natural man, who does not perceive the things of God, sees outwardly in these visible creatures the appearance but does not inwardly understand the reason. But he who is spiritual and can judge all things, while he considers outwardly the beauty of the work, inwardly conceives how marvelous is the wisdom of the Creator.

St. Bonaventura, who died within Dante's lifetime and who has also a prominent place among the saints of Dante's Heaven, expresses the same idea in his *Breviloquium:*

... *Primum principium fecit mundum istum sensibilem ad declarandum seipsum, videlicet ut homo per illum tanquam per speculum et vestigium, reduceretur in Deum artificem amandum et laudandum. Et secundum hoc duplex est liber, unus scilicet scriptus intus, qui est Dei aeterna ars et sapientia, et alius scriptus foris, scilicet mundus sensibilis.*

... the first source made this visible world to declare himself, namely, so that man, through it as by a mirror and by traces, might be brought to love and praise God the author. And accordingly the book is two-fold, one, that is, written within, which is the eternal art and wisdom of God, and the other written without, that is, the visible world.

This, then, is that same volume which the prophet Ezekiel saw written within and without. But what the prophet saw as one book, St. Bonaventura, for purposes of a concept which is being squared with what is ultimately a Platonic view, has seen as two. And his first and inner volume is, in turn, that which Dante sees, at the end of *Paradiso* (xxxiii, 85-87), when he gazes at last into the Eternal Light:

> *Nel suo profondo vidi che s'interna,*
> *legato con amore in un volume,*
> *ciò che per l'universo si squaderna.*

In its depths I saw ingathering, bound with love in one volume, what throughout the universe is scattered quires.

In place of one volume, two—to express that view of the world which sees things here below as but a pale copy of the things that are above; a view which in Hugh and Bonaventura and Dante was nurtured on the Platonism of St. Augustine and ultimately on that of St. Paul. In fact, the text so often cited in support of the whole doctrine is in Paul's lettter to the Romans (I, 18-20):

> For the wrath of God is revealed from heaven against all ungodliness and unrighteousness of men, who hold the truth in unrighteousness; because that which may be known of God is manifest in them; for God hath shewed it unto them. *For the invisible things of him from the creation of the world are clearly seen, being understood by the things that are made,* even his eternal power and Godhead; so that they are without excuse.

But that the figure of a book should be found appropriate to express the nature of a world revealing a creator's intention arises, no doubt, by analogy with that other book of which God is also the author and which is literally a book: I mean Holy Scripture. Almost never is the Book of the Universe mentioned without the other, the Bible, coming into the picture. Both "books," we are commonly told, are spread open before the eyes of men that they may read and that their minds may be turned to the Author of both. Each book is a revelation of the hidden truths of His Providence. Both books are given to man for his salvation.

At the beginning of his *Summa theologica,* Thomas Aquinas has made a brief defense of the multiple meaning of words in Holy Scripture. His statement of the matter affords an excellent glimpse of the conceptual tie which bound the one of these books of God to the other, explaining as it does how, in both books, the word of God is necessarily different from the words of men:

> The author of Holy Writ is God in whose power it is to signify His meaning, not by words only (as man also can do) but also by things themselves . . . Therefore that first signification whereby words signify things belongs to the first sense, the historical or literal. That signification whereby things signified by words have themselves also a signification is called the spiritual sense.

It is because things of the real world are themselves signs that they may be seen as so many words; and it is because when taken together they have a syntax and total meaning that they may be

said to make up a book. Things are such "words" as only God has
the power to use. And this means events moving in time as well
as things taken statically. Time itself, in fact, and the unfolding of
events in time, is of the essence of the Book of the Universe. History too is a revelation, the revelation of the intention of an Author,
as St. Augustine tells us in his treatise *On Christian Doctrine:*

And even when in the course of an historical narrative former institutions of men are described, the history itself is not to be reckoned
among human institutions; because things that are past and gone and
cannot be undone are to be reckoned as belonging to the course of time
of which God is the author and governor.

We are not good readers of the *Vita Nuova* for having forgotten
these ways of looking on the world about us, for in our forgetfulness the metaphor of a Book of Memory in the *Vita Nuova* can
seem something new and uncalled-for; and the gloss on the number
nine in chapter xxix can likewise seem something forced into that
book by a willful and superstitious mind. But in the light of what
we have now recalled and the tradition which we have thus sampled
at various points, we may see how far wrong we should be to
take it so.

Nor must we forget that both the Book of Creation and the Bible
are revelations. To the eye of a competent reader both are capable
of disclosing a truth of divine origin. But precisely because of this
and because of the Author which they have, no human eye will ever
see all the meaning that there is in those texts. For, as another passage from St. Paul may remind us, we see through a glass darkly,
while we walk in this life. And by the very nature of the revelation
made by these books, there will always be some uncertainty and
obscurity. The reader of either book will always have to allow for
that better reader who might be able to see more deeply into the
mystery or more subtly into the truth that is hidden than he. Thus,
for example, Augustine on the hidden and spiritual meaning of the
Exodus:

But they [the Egyptians] gave their gold and their silver and their
garments to the people of God as they were going out of Egypt, not
knowing how the things they gave would be turned to the service of

Christ. For what was done at the time of the Exodus was no doubt a type prefiguring what happens now. *And this I say without prejudice to any other interpretation that may be as good or better.*

We may let Augustine's gloss bring us back to the *Vita Nuova*. It can remind us that the scribe of the Book of Memory, as the final remark of his own gloss shows, is reading his text in much the same way as Augustine was reading the word of God:

> *Dunque se lo tre è fattore per se medesimo del nove, e lo fattore per se medesimo de li miracoli è tre, cioè Padre e Figlio e Spirito Santo, li quali sono tre e uno, questa donna fue accompagnata da questo numero del nove a dare ad intendere ch'ella era uno nove, cioè uno miracolo, la cui radice, cioè del miracolo, è solamente la mirabile Trinitade. Forse ancora per più sottile persona si vederebbe in ciò più sottile ragione; ma questa è quella ch'io ne veggio, e che più mi piace.*

Therefore, since three is the maker by itself of nine and the maker by itself of miracles is three, that is, Father and Son and Holy Ghost, which are three and one, this lady was accompanied by this number nine in order to signify that she was a nine, that is, a miracle, whose root, that is, of the miracle, is only the marvelous Trinity. *Perhaps a more subtle person would see in that a more subtle reason; but this is the one which I see in it and which I like best.*

Augustine was reading words written into one book of God, the Bible. The scribe of the *Vita Nuova,* when he reads the prose surrounding his poems, is reading words from God's other book, the Book of the Universe. Here, then, are events which were "words" even before they took their place in a Book of Memory. Only because these "words" are words of God can this scribe's gloss find a hidden meaning in them. And only when we in turn have understood that his way of reading these words is an established way shall we see that when he is writing his gloss on the miracle that Beatrice was, he is doing a reasonable thing.

*

*   *

Quite a large part of the *Vita Nuova* is reasonable. At least, almost everything outside of the poems is reasoned. The prose of the *Vita Nuova* is addressed to a reasonable reader.

It is a prose which seems sometimes to proceed almost by syllogism. One may take, for example, that passage which explains how Beatrice must necessarily have been sad at the death of her father (chapter XXII):

Appresso ciò non molti dì passati, sì come piacque al glorioso sire lo quale non negoe la morte a sè, colui che era stato genitore di tanta maraviglia quanta si vedea ch'era questa nobilissima Beatrice, di questa vita uscendo, a la gloria etternale se ne gio veracemente. Onde con ciò sia cosa che cotale partire sia doloroso a coloro che rimangono e sono stati amici di colui che se ne va; e nulla sia sì intima amistade come da buon padre a buon figliuolo e da buon figliuolo a buon padre; e questa donna fosse in altissimo grado di bontade, e lo suo padre, sì come da molti si crede e vero è, fosse bono in alto grado; manifesto è che questa donna fue amarissimamente piena di dolore.

Not many days after this, even as it pleased the glorious Lord who did not deny himself death, he who had been the begetter of such a marvel as this most noble Beatrice was seen to be, leaving this life, departed to eternal glory. Wherefore inasmuch as such a departure is grievous to those who remain and have been friends of him who departs; and no friendship is so intimate as that of a good father toward a good child and of a good child to a good father; and this lady was of the highest degree of goodness, and her father, as many believe and as is true, was good in a high degree; it is evident that this lady was most bitterly filled with grief.

All of those passages in prose in the *Vita Nuova* which carry the burden of the narrative from poem to poem are called *ragioni,* reasons. And, indeed, if they were all like the above they would appear to deserve that name even in a modern sense. But by no means all the prose is reasoned in that way. Yet all connecting narrative passages are spoken of as *ragioni.* It seems necessary to understand why this is so.

But let us recognize first that besides that prose which is the narrative there is also a prose of another sort coming between the poems. These are passages bearing still another name. They are called "divisions." These follow their respective poems in the first half of the book and precede them in the second half. They are written by the poet to point out the parts and the order of the parts in each poem. The longer the poem, the longer the division. These divisions, moreover, are in the present tense, that is, are written *now* into the copy which the scribe who is the poet is making.

One example will serve to remind any reader of them all. The following is only the first part of the division given for the first of the *canzoni* (chapter xix):

Questa canzone, acciò che sia meglio intesa, la dividerò più artificiosamente che l'altre cose di sopra. E però prima ne fo tre parti: la prima parte è proemio de le sequenti parole; la seconda è lo intento trattato; la terza è quasi una serviziale de le precedenti parole. La seconda comincia quivi: Angelo clama; *la terza quivi:* Canzone, io so che. *La prima parte si divide in quattro: ne la prima dico a cu'io dicer voglio de la mia donna, e perchè io voglio dire; ne la seconda dico quale me pare avere a me stesso quand'io penso lo suo valore, e com'io direi s'io non perdessi l'ardimento; ne la terza dico come credo dire di lei, acciò ch'io non sia impedito da viltà; ne la quarta, ridicendo anche a cui ne intenda dire, dico la cagione per che dico a loro. La seconda comincia quivi:* Io dico; *la terza quivi:* E io non vo'parlar; *la quarta:* donne e donzelle. *Poscia quando dico:* Angelo clama, *comincio a trattare di questa donna.*

In order that this *canzone* may be better understood, I will divide it more elaborately than the other things above. And hence I make three parts of it: the first part is a proem to the following words; the second is the intended treatise; the third is as a handmaiden to the preceding words. The second begins here: *Angelo clama;* the third here: *Canzone, io so che.* The first part is divided in four: in the first I say to whom I wish to speak of my lady, and wherefore I wish to speak; in the second I say what I myself seem to experience when I think on her worthiness, and how I should write of her if I did not lose courage; in the third I say how I mean to write of her so that I be not impeded by faintheartedness; in the fourth, saying again for whom I intend to write of this, I give the reason why I speak to them. The second begins here: *Io dico;* the third here; *E io non vo'parlar;* the fourth: *donne e donzelle.* Then when I say *Angelo clama,* I begin to treat of this lady.

With every poem in the *Vita Nuova,* either some such division of the parts is given or some reason is given as to why it may be dispensed with. In the second half of the book, the divisions are more frequently omitted than in the first. But even in the first part they are sometimes omitted; in which cases, the reasons given for this serve to make clear just what the purpose of the divisions is. Thus, after the sonnet on the *gabbo* (chapter xiv), the poet writes:

> *Questo sonetto non divido in parti, però che la divisione non si fa se non per aprire la sentenzia de la cosa divisa; onde con ciò sia cosa che per la sua ragionata cagione assai sia manifesto, non ha mestiere di divisione.*

This sonnet I do not divide into parts, since a division is only made to open up the meaning of the thing divided; wherefore, inasmuch as this one is made clear enough by its narrated cause, it has no need of a division.

Or, the poet may give the division of a poem up to a certain point only and then go no further into the parts of the poem for reasons which again clearly reveal the conceived purpose of these little *explications de texte:* as, for instance, in the closing words of the division to the first *canzone:*

> *Dico bene che, a più aprire lo intendimento di questa canzone, si converrebbe usare di più minute divisioni; ma tuttavia chi non è di tanto ingegno che per queste che sono fatte la possa intendere, a me non dispiace se la mi lascia stare, chè certo io temo d'avere a troppi comunicato lo suo intendimento pur per queste divisioni che fatte sono, s'elli avvenisse che molti le potessero audire.*

I admit that to further disclose the meaning of this *canzone* it would be necessary to use even more minute divisions; but still, whoever is not clever enough to understand it with those [divisions] that are given [above], I shall not be sorry if he lets it be, for certainly I fear to have divulged its meaning to too many persons even with these divisions that have been made, should it happen that many should hear them.

Evidently, the poems of the *Vita Nuova* were not written for many readers. This the reader is told many times over. Those only are to read or to hear who have intelligence of love. Even so, the modern reader will more readily resign himself to this exclusiveness than he will accept the need for the divisions. For by the time he has come to a poem through the prose narrative which precedes it, so that the poem itself seems a kind of restatement of what has been told already in prose, he cannot but feel that another review of the poem in a division is completely uncalled for. He likes to think of himself as having enough intelligence to dispense with this last gloss to the poem; and no doubt he has. In short, what is said of that sonnet on the *gabbo* would seem to express for him what he feels to be the general redundancy of all the divisions:

> *Onde con ciò sia cosa che per la sua ragionata cagione assai sia mani-festo, non ha mestiere di divisione.*

Wherefore, inasmuch as this one [the poem] is made clear enough by its narrated cause, it has no need of a division.

Giovanni Boccaccio must also have felt this about the divisions, since in his edition of the *Vita Nuova* he simply omitted them.

Why then do we have them?

The answer is given repeatedly in the *Vita Nuova:* a division serves to open up the *sentenzia* or the *intendimento* of a poem—the substance, that is, and the intention of what the poem says.

*

*   *

But I think that we shall neither understand the presence of the divisions in the *Vita Nuova* nor see how they are a part of the metaphor of the Book of Memory unless we are willing to accept the fact that one's way of looking at a poem may be an "imitation" of his way of looking at the world; and this for the very good reason that a poem may be or perhaps ought to be an imitation of the world. To help us at least to allow such a view of poetry, we may need to recall what we have already learned to see: that to the contemplative eye of man in the Middle Ages the world revealed an order and a harmony which it was not possible that it should not have, having the Creator that it had; that the world might even be seen as a book written by God, because like that other book of God, the Bible, the creation was addressed to man. In either case, man is the reader. The Book of the World is written for him.

But for what part of him? First of all, for his senses. But not for his senses alone. Let us remember what Hugh of St. Victor has said about the reader of the Book of the World who stopped with the senses. He was an illiterate and foolish man:

Quemadmodum autem si illiteratus quis apertum librum videat,
figuras aspicit, litteras non cognoscit: ita stultus et animalis homo qui
non percipit ea quae Dei sunt in visibilibus istis creaturis foris videt
speciem sed intus non intelligit rationem.

But just as some illiterate man who sees an open book, looks at the
figures, but does not recognize the letters: just so the foolish and natural
man, who does not perceive the things of God, sees outwardly in these
visible creatures the appearance but does not inwardly understand the
reason.

The reader of the *Vita Nuova* will do well to have this view of
the world in mind when he asks why there are divisions and, indeed,
why there is any of the reasoned prose at all around the poems.

The Book of the World is not addressed alone to the senses of
man, although the senses must perforce be the way by which it first
speaks to him. Behind what the eye sees, further in (*intus*), is a
meaning addressed to a faculty of man more noble than his senses:
his reason—an endowment which makes him much more than an
animal and something a little less than an angel. Just so a poem.
Like the world of which it is in some way an imitation, a poem
speaks first of all to the senses. But *intus,* further in, a poem will
be found to speak to the reason. Like the world, a poem has a
rational structure. And because of this, the reader is not a good
reader who does not discover that what is delectable in the sensuous
order is also intelligible in the rational order, that the harmony and
order of the parts of a poem may speak to a faculty capable of
digesting the sensible in terms of a rational understanding.

To such a legitimate and indeed indispensable part of the enjoyment of a poem, the divisions in the *Vita Nuova* mean to contribute. One should not overlook the verb *aprire* (to open), which is
repeatedly used to say what the divisions are intended to do. The
intention and substance of a poem, that part of a poem which
reason can use, is conceived of as being on the inside of a poem
(*intus*), and a division serves to "open up" the poem so that reason
may lay hold of that substance.

In a similar spirit, the gloss to Holy Scripture sought to "open
up" the meaning of the words of God. It was with the same intention that the scientist of the Middle Ages looked to those words of

God which the things of nature are. Now the work of poets ought to resemble the work of God, ought, like His creation, to be addressed to a reasonable reader and be susceptible of the same exegetical methods.

The analogy, however, goes further than that.

Not only should poems reveal a structure in "imitation" of the creation of God, but poets are or ought to be like God. This, at least, I would suggest to be the proper approach to an argument in chapter xxv of the *Vita Nuova,* which in part we have already seen and to which we do well at this point to return.

This is that chapter where, one remembers, the scribe of the Book of Memory breaks off his copying and steps out on the stage himself. He is the author of the poems. For what is done in them he is responsible, and he has wished here to anticipate and to answer a criticism which is certain to come, he feels, from the right kind of reader: from just such a reasonable reader as ought to be reading his poems. Even before this point, the poet had shown that he was aware of the likely presence of such a desirable reader when, after the *ballata* in chapter xii (in which he had addressed the *ballata* itself as if it were capable of hearing), he wrote:

Potrebbe già l'uomo opporre contra me e dicere che non sapesse a cui fosse lo mio parlare in seconda persona, però che la ballata non è altro che queste parole ched io parlo: e però dico che questo dubbio io lo intendo solvere e dichiarare in questo libello ancora in parte più dubbiosa; e allora intenda qui chi qui dubita, o chi qui volesse opporre in questo modo.

Someone indeed might make objection to me and say that he did not know to whom I spoke in the second person, since the *ballata* is nothing save these words which I speak; wherefore I say that this doubt I intend to solve and explain in this little book in a part even more dubious; and so let him look to that point who has doubts here, or whoever might wish to make any such objection.

The more "dubious" part has now come. In chapter xxiv the poet has written a poem in which he has presented Love as if Love were a person. In the poem Love is said to walk and talk and laugh. Now the reasonable reader will wonder here, just as he wondered about addressing the *ballata,* how Love can really do any such thing

as this. Is it really true that Love is a person? Or, to put it more
philosophically, that Love is a substance?

The poet has devoted his chapter xxv to the answer: No. In
truth, Love is no person and no substance. The truth is that Love
is only an accident (passions are accidents) occurring in persons
(and persons are substances).

But how now? May poets write untruths?

The answer cannot be a simple yes or no. It is that the ancient
poets spoke in such figures and used rhetorical colors (they used,
that is, personification and figurative language); and what the ancient poets did, modern poets have a right to do. But let no ignorant
person grow insolent over such a thing as this! Let him know
rather that the ancients did not use the figures of poetry without
reason—nor may modern poets do so:

*E acciò che non ne pigli alcuna baldanza persona grossa, dico che
nè li poete parlavano così sanza ragione, nè quelli che rimano deono
parlare così non avendo alcuno ragionamento in loro di quello che
dicono; però che grande vergogna sarebbe a colui che rimasse cose sotto
vesta di figura o di colore rettorico, e poscia, domandato, non sapesse
denudare le sue parole da cotale vesta, in guisa che avessero verace intendimento. E questo mio primo amico e io ne sapemo bene di quelli
che così rimano stoltamente.*

And in order that no ignorant person may grow arrogant over this,
I say that neither the ancient poets spoke thus without reason nor must
those who write in rhyme speak so, having no reasoning in them of
what they write; for it would be a great shame to one who wrote in
rhyme of things under the garb of figure and rhetorical color and then,
when asked, could not divest his words of such a garb so that they
might have true meaning. And this first friend of mine and I know
well of some who write in rhyme thus foolishly.

The argument of this whole chapter has been taken by some to
be the statement of a doctrine of allegory. This is a mistake. To
define Love as an accident in a substance is not to proclaim an
allegorical meaning for Love, but is rather to show that when a poet
writes of love in figure and rhetorical color he knows (or ought to
know) what the truth is behind the figure and color.

The argument here, however, is of extreme interest for what it

conceives the nature of poetry to be; or better, perhaps, for what
it insists that the nature of poets be. This now is quite another concept than that which spoke of "opening up" a poem. A division was
designed to "open" a poem, and what it disclosed was, so to speak,
in the poem itself—was its *sentenzia*, its substance. But the truth
about love is not in the poem. It transcends the poem. It is (or
ought to be) in the mind of the poet. This particular argument is
therefore more interesting for what it says about poets than poems.

Just as poems ought to resemble the creation, as we have seen,
so poets ought to be like God. The world created by God is transcended by the Truth which is in Himself. Let us recall what Bonaventura said about the Book of the Created World:

. . . *duplex est liber, unus scilicet scriptus intus, qui est Dei aeterna ars
et sapientia, et alius scriptus foris, scilicet mundus sensibilis.*

. . . the book is twofold, one, that is, written within, which is the eternal
art and wisdom of God, and the other written without, that is, the
visible world.

So it should be with poets. Their art and wisdom should tran-
scend their little creations in figure and color. In their minds should
be the reasons for their creations. They ought, in short, to work
in the image of God.

No resemblance in this sense may obscure, to be sure, the infinite
difference. For one thing, God is not accountable and poets are.
God may not be asked to say what the Truth about His creation is.
Poets may be asked for the truth about theirs. And if they are
asked, then it should be a great shame to any one of them if he were
unable to show that, over and above his creation in figure and color,
he knew the truth of his work.

Thus, not only is the reader of a poem expected to be a reasonable reader, but the creator of a poem is under the obligation to be
reasonable too.

*
*   *

To think further on the difference between the poet and his
exemplar who is God is to see that not only is he unlike God in
being responsible to others for what he does; but he is also, of course,

a creature contained by the events and circumstances of time; a creator, to be sure, but one whose little creations arise out of such events and circumstances and find their causes in them. A poem, that is, does not come solely from the mind of the poet. It arises out of the poet's experience in the world. Or there is perhaps this better way to state it: the figures of a poem have their reason in the poet's mind; but poems have their causes in the real world.

May not these causes be called the *reasons* of the poems? They are so called in the *Vita Nuova*. And this makes for no particular difficulty in the modern reader's mind. He quite commonly uses the words "cause" and "reason" as synonymous. But it may be that in the usage of the *Vita Nuova* there is more than this loose synonymity.

We have seen that an account of the circumstances in which a poem arose may obviate the necessity for "dividing" it; that the reasoning of the "cause" might supplant the reasoning of a division. The poet has said as much when he explained that for a certain poem he would not give a division,

però che la divisione non si fa se non per aprire la sentenzia de la cosa divisa; onde con ciò sia cosa che per la sua ragionata cagione assai sia manifesto, non ha mestiere di divisione.

since a division is only made to open up the meaning of the thing divided; wherefore, inasmuch as this one [the poem] is made clear enough by its reasoned cause, it has no need of a division.

Ragionata cagione, a reasoned cause. This, then, is the proper name for the passages in prose which surround the poems in the Book of Memory and tell how those poems came to be. It seems a fitting name indeed, for those passages do give the causes of the poems. In a sense, they might be said to be *cagioni,* causes, themselves. But they may also be said to be *ragioni,* reasons, in that they are an account of the causes. The verb *ragionare* can mean both "to narrate" and "to reason" and does so here in the *Vita Nuova,* especially where the narration is addressed to a reasonable reader. We see, thus, how a cause is also a reason. A cause that is narrated or reasoned, a *ragionata cagione,* is a reason.

But all this appears idle indeed until one sees that within the metaphor of the Book of Memory the word *ragione* makes sense, and that to make sense there it must result from just such semantic steps.

One must know, first of all, that the word *ragione,* even without having a context in the image of a Book of Memory, can mean "explanation" or "commentary." We may see this in the Provençal use of the same word (*razo*) in manuscripts of troubador poetry, where it designates certain short accounts in prose which explain the occasion of a poem. Already in these Provençal collections of poems, and without any such image as that of a book of memory, the word *razo* means "gloss," just as it means "gloss" in the *Vita Nuova.* But how much more appropriately it can have this meaning in the *Vita Nuova!* For an initial image of the Book of Memory already calls for such a meaning. And, because of this, the *ragioni* of the *Vita Nuova* can stand as glosses in a quite literal sense.

*

*   *

What, then, is the whole picture of this copy from the Book of Memory as it is developed from the image in the Proem?

It is indeed clear enough that one might even translate it to a page of manuscript and give it a graphic representation in the mere arrangement of the words on the page, causing to appear in different handwriting, for instance, those parts which are done by different authors or at different times. For we should realize that a reader in Dante's time who turned the manuscript pages of the *Vita Nuova* would already have guessed, even before he began to read, what the Proem and the later development of the image there will but confirm, namely, that here must be the text of a certain number of poems around which someone has written a gloss in prose. He would feel at once that the Proem confirms this first impression. The original from which this scribe will copy is a book. And as one reads on in the copy, it is plain that under the rubric INCIPIT VITA NOVA the original book contains poems, and around the poems passages in prose which are the *ragioni,* the commentary to the poems. There is, of course, no way for any reader to examine the original

Book of Memory, and hence no way of knowing whether in the manuscript the handwriting itself may have revealed the fact that the author of the poems was not the same person as the author of this prose gloss. But that this is the case is evident from what is said here and there as one reads on. For the author of the poems is now become the copyist of the Book of Memory, and it is quite clear at more than one point that he is able to scrutinize the prose he finds there as something written by a hand not his own, indeed, not by human hand at all.

So much for the original of the Book of Memory.

But this scribe does not only copy. He makes additions to the original. So that, were this literally such a page of manuscript as we are imagining it to be, what the scribe now adds would appear in the copy in a later hand, a hand which might conceivably show a resemblance to that earlier hand which wrote the poems (since this is the poet's in both cases), but would in no way resemble the hand that wrote the *ragioni* in prose.

The scribe's additions to the original are these:

To his poems he adds a gloss which says how they are to be divided. This gloss he calls the divisions.

He adds a note on his practice as poet which becomes the twenty-fifth chapter of his copy.

To the original gloss in prose he adds a gloss of his own, examples of which are his chapter xi on the marvelous virtue of the greeting of Beatrice, and his chapter xxix on the number nine.

That is the whole picture: a text of poems with a gloss and then yet another gloss. Such a book would in no way have troubled a reader of the thirteenth century. The margins of his manuscripts were filled with just such a multiple gloss, and he might well have read Holy Scriptures, codices of canon and civil law, the works of Aristotle, and Vergil's *Aeneid,* for instance, in editions much like this.

All of which means that the metaphor of a Book of Memory, as the *Vita Nuova* uses it, was under no strain of novelty, and that the image provided a very good way of telling a reasonable reader what he would want to know about certain poems.

But the validity of that image as a part of a work of art extends beyond that: for these pages of a Book of Memory, already filled with a prose not written by human hand, give foundation to the presence of mysteries; and this scribe making his copy, and poring over the pages, and finding new meaning in them, makes the revelation itself of those mysteries possible by providing for an eye that can see them and a time when they may be seen.

III

From Love to Caritas

In order to see the intention of an author in the prose narrative of the *Vita Nuova,* one is obliged to take a position outside of the metaphor of the Book of Memory and the implications of that metaphor. Seen from the inside, this narrative of past events is a gloss which may not be attributed to human authorship at all. But the metaphor would not be a metaphor if it had no outside. If this narrative were literally such a gloss, we might not speak of the *Vita Nuova* as a work of art, since a work of art postulates, first of all, an author's intention and what may be called a strategy, which is simply the author's way of reaching his end. But one may surely assume that, in this regard, and at a point this far along in our inquiry, there is no need to plead the case of the *Vita Nuova.* We are not now likely to take the symmetry of the Book of Memory for an accident. The way in which the death of Beatrice appears (and reappears) at its center, the manner in which this Book becomes a book with a multiple gloss revealing the true meaning of her life and death (and the causes and the meaning of the poems)— these are all so many indications of a construction which is ever aware of the inner principle of its own being, which is a principle of becoming toward an end.

But there is one aspect of its becoming which may not be grasped without turning from these more strictly formal outlines to what has more to do with the conceptual content of the work. Not that we may think of a content in the *Vita Nuova* as existing in separation from a form. The "content" we would here distinguish is only another aspect of form, and works hand in hand with the death of Beatrice and the revelations of the Book of Memory to make a whole. It is, like these other things, part of a total dialectic making a single articulation.

To consider this one aspect of its form for the moment as something apart is to see that the action of the *Vita Nuova* exists on more than one level, and that it may rightly be said to describe another kind of circle than that which we have so far noticed centering on the death of Beatrice. The action, in this, makes another kind of movement forward, a movement having its beginning not in Beatrice's death but in a certain conception of love. And whereas the articulation of the first line of action is by means of a progressive revelation of the miraculous nature of Beatrice, this other has its being in a gradual disclosure of the true nature of love. These may in the end prove to be essentially one and the same line. At this point we may at least see that along the second of these, Love itself can be observed to undergo a transformation, revealing itself to be always something more than it had at first seemed to be. And the direction is always upward. But only by a close attention to detail will we see it as upward at all; or even glimpse, indeed, the further fact that there is, in this conceptual sense, a downward direction to love also. For it is with this second line as it is with the other: the current is alternating. At the last we realize that, in and from the beginning, the idea of love met at the end had been present all the while, informing the whole development of the story: we learn, in short, that the pattern of yet another circle has been built into the structure of the *Vita Nuova.*

This we begin most clearly to see at a point again near the center of the *Vita Nuova,* a point made salient by the disappearance of one of the main characters from the stage. Since that stage, so to speak, is so small and has so few actors upon it, the removal of even one of these must be an event of no little prominence. For there are, after all, only three main characters in this little drama of love: madonna Beatrice, the poet, and the God of Love. Madonna and the poet remain in the action to the end. But the God of Love quits the stage at a halfway point in the book, not to return again. As a person in the prose narrative he is last seen in chapter xxiv.

It is a chapter which has already claimed some special attention from us, for in it the God of Love (speaking in the poet's heart) pointed out the analogy of Beatrice and the lady whose name was Giovanna to Christ and John the Baptist. But what we did not then note and what proves now to be especially significant is that immediately following the assertion of that analogy, the God had added:

E chi volesse sottilmente considerare, quella Beatrice chiamerebbe Amore per molta simiglianza che ha meco.

And whoever should consider subtly would call that Beatrice *Love* because of the great resemblance which she has to me.

Of course, in a sense, one had always been ready to see Beatrice as *Love* and to understand that Love as a God was after all only the sign of a power, that he had no real existence as she had. But when it turns out that beyond this point in the story the God of Love does not again appear as a character in the prose, then the above words will be seen as a kind of farewell speech on his part: something like a last will, delegating to Beatrice henceforth all the authority of Love. No longer will the sign of the power of a passion be other than the object and agent itself of that passion. Love, the conception of love, is undergoing a change. Anyone who is capable of looking subtly at the matter will see now that Love is Beatrice. By such a pronouncement the God of Love might almost be said to have removed himself from the stage. By his own words, he is declared surplus.

This fact is confirmed by subsequent developments in the story and, in truth, can be seen clearly only in retrospect, from the end. From that point, too, one will be able to observe that it is not only this twenty-fourth chapter which has aimed at the removal of the God from the narrative action, but the following chapter as well. In this there is a strategy quite subtle and delightful to discover. The reader will remember how that following chapter, the twenty-fifth, is a poet's gloss to his practice as a poet; how there the poet had explained that Love is no person really, but is only an accident in a substance. He will also recall that, strictly in terms of the image given by the Proem, this gloss did not concern Love as Love had appeared in the prose but only as he was in the verse. But now, when such a chapter as this twenty-fifth, bringing into question the reality of Love as a person, follows hard on one in which the God has pronounced, as it were, his own end, we know that in yet a deeper sense the gloss of chapter xxv is part of a total strategy aimed at attaining in the prose a new conceptual position regarding Love.

Not that we are now called upon to violate the terms of the image of the Book of Memory which we had learned to respect. It is only that for the moment we have taken a position here outside of the metaphor of the Book of Memory in order to observe an author's intention. Now, having done this, if we try to imagine what effect it would have had upon us had Love as a God (and as a person) appeared again in the prose beyond chapter xxv, we realize that we should have found the "reality" of the God (that reality which even appearance in art must have) so seriously undermined that our feeling toward the "reality" of all the events in the prose beyond that point would have been affected. Even in the prose, indeed, especially in the prose, it cannot be the same with the God of Love after the poet's gloss of chapter xxv. In the verse, Love as a passion may be the figure and fiction that he is declared by that gloss to be. But in the prose, that is, among those "words" which are things and real events, he may not, beyond the gloss of chapter xxv, again command the credence from us that he did before that gloss.

Along one line of the action (as we have seen) there had come a time when pretenses were to be put aside. Beatrice was soon to die. Now comes a time along this other line when the God of Love must be thrust aside. For our direction is upward, and we leave old positions for new. And the God of Love is very much the sign of an old position.

*

*   *

He is this in a way which we shall have to look beyond the *Vita Nuova* itself in order to see. Beatrice belongs to the private world of the *Vita Nuova*. So does the poet. But the God of Love has a public existence. He belongs to a tradition. He is the sign of a tradition. His meaning is as much outside the *Vita Nuova* as inside.

To examine this tradition might seem to lead us away from the work in hand and to lose us in literary history. But the fact is that in the twenty-fifth chapter itself there is a standing invitation to become aware of just this tradition. For there the poet has found the occasion to remind us of the convention within which he, as a modern poet, is writing. It is, he says, not very old; and, incidentally, in saying this he advances a curious reason why anyone should ever have written poems of love in a language not Latin, and at the same time shows himself to be a very reactionary young man, maintaining as he does that since modern poetry began as love poetry, no one should write in rhyme on any other subject:

A cotale cosa dichiarare, secondo che è buono a presente, prima è da intendere che anticamente non erano dicitori d'amore in lingua volgare, anzi erano dicitori d'amore certi poete in lingua latina . . . E non è molto numero d'anni passati, che appariro prima questi poete volgari; chè dire per rima in volgare tanto è quanto dire per versi in latino, secondo alcuna proporzione. E segno che sia picciolo tempo, è che se volemo cercare in lingua d'oco e in quella di sì, noi non troviamo cose dette anzi lo presente tempo per cento e cinquanta anni. E la cagione per che alquanti grossi ebbero fama di sapere dire, è che quasi fuoro li primi che dissero in lingua di sì. E lo primo che cominciò a dire sì come poeta volgare, si mosse però che volle fare intendere le sue parole a donna, a la quale era malagevole d'intendere li versi latini. E questo è contra coloro che rimano sopra altra matera che amorosa, con ciò sia cosa che cotale modo di parlare fosse dal principio trovato per dire d'amore.

To explain which matter, in so far as it is here fitting, first one should know that in olden times there were none who wrote of love in the vulgar tongue, rather those who wrote of love were certain poets in the Latin tongue . . . And it is not many years ago that these poets in the vulgar tongue first appeared; for to compose in rhyme in the vulgar tongue is equivalent in some proportion to composing in verses in Latin. And the sign that it is a short time is that if we will seek in Provençal and in Italian we do not find anything composed more than one hundred and fifty years before the present time. And the reason why some few crude persons won fame for knowing how to write is that they were almost the first to compose anything in Italian. And the first one to write as a poet in the vulgar tongue did so because he wished to have a lady understand his words for whom it was difficult to understand verses in Latin. And this is against those who write in rhyme on any theme that is not amorous, inasmuch as such a way of writing was in the beginning devised in order to write of love.

The tradition is the lyric tradition of Provence. This kind of poetry, which according to the poet is only a century and a half old, began with the troubadours. All readers of the *Vita Nuova* will doubtless know something about it. They would always be better readers if they knew more. This much at least is indispensable: the awareness that the God of Love with his faithful subjects, who are all poets, and these poets each with his madonna to worship and to extol in verse, are the sure signs of that tradition (which is somewhat older than the poet tells us it is); that modern love poetry does begin with this tradition; and that the beginning of the *Vita Nuova,* with just such a God and with his faithful subjects who are poets, and with a lady whose name may be spelled *beatrice* as well as Beatrice, has its proper context in that tradition. Of course, the more familiar the reader is with the poetry of the troubadours the more he will recognize the signs of this latter fact. He will be more likely to see that especially the first poems of this book are very much in the manner of Provence. He will know that the way in which Love appears to the poet, the way madonna is seen and approached through the poems, the "screen-ladies," and the whole ritual and cult of love to which only the elect may be admitted—that all this in Dante's time has a public meaning outside of the *Vita Nuova* because it is part of an established convention. On the other hand, he may not know all of these things; and still, if he is aware only of the one fact that such a beginning has public significance, he is prepared to see the larger meaning of the disappearance of the God of Love at the halfway point in the book.

But if the removal of the God of Love from the stage of the *Vita Nuova* is the abandoning of an old position for a new, what is this new one? Does it too, like the old, have an established and public existence?

It does. A modern reader, however, is even less likely to be familiar with it. It is a position in theology. It has to do with a conception of love held by saints and mystics such as St. Augustine and St. Bernard of Clairvaux. What the position was it is worth our while to attempt to understand. Unless we do, we may be aware that the *Vita Nuova* is "going somewhere," we may even know that in such chapters as the twenty-fourth and twenty-fifth it is moving toward a new conception of love, but we shall not be prepared to know when it arrives at its goal.

The *Divine Comedy* in itself can tell us what saints and mystics and Christian theologians thought of love. Love is God. God is love. God's love moves the sun and all the stars. It moves the whole created universe, and that universe is itself suspended from a single act of love. For the act which ended in the Creation had its beginning in a movement of love. Both the physical and moral world have their origin and cause in love. Our Redemption is an act of love which began first of all in God. Through love we return from the exile of this earth to God. Love is the primary motive force in every created thing, be it a stone or an angel.

A reader of the *Comedy* would thus have no need to reread the *Confessions* of St. Augustine to be reminded of these things; but from certain passages of that earlier work on love he will remember how love, even as the *Comedy* tells us, is the weight within each of us bearing us upward to our final place of rest in God:

In Thy gift we rest; then we enjoy Thee. Our rest is Thy gift, our life's place. Love lifts us up thither, and Thy good spirit advances our lowliness from the gates of death. In Thy good pleasure lies our peace. Weight makes not downward only but to its own place also. Fire mounts upward, a stone sinks downward. All things pressed by their own weight go towards their proper places. Oil poured in the bottom of the water is raised above it; water poured upon oil sinks to the bottom of the oil. They are driven by their own weights, to seek their own place. Things a little out of their places become unquiet; put them in their order again and they are quieted. My weight is my love: by that am I carried, whithersoever I be carried. We are inflamed by Thy gift and are carried upwards: we wax hot within and we go on. We ascend the ways that be in our heart, and we sing a song of degrees.

But about this love which bears us up to God and which is also known as charity we have more subtle truths than these to learn. For if we are aware that God is love (*Deus caritas est*) according to the truth as revealed in the Fourth Gospel, we must also know that this love which is God is substantial love, and that love as a substance can be only in God. God is love. But this substantial love is solely the love of the Father for the Son and the love of the

Son for the Father, and this Love is no other than the third person of the Blessed Trinity. This is Eternal Love which would have been even had there never been a creation to participate in it. The Creation is an overflowing of this love, and all created things therefore live and move by love. In love, which is first of all in God, all creatures participate. From Him they receive this love as a gift—and this gift is charity. If they have charity, therefore, they have it by participation, they have it as an accident.

At least to understand the matter in these terms is to understand it with St. Bernard. He, to be sure, is only one of a chorus of voices telling us these things. But since Bernard, being so learned in charity, becomes Dante's last guide to the Beatific Vision of *Paradiso,* we may with special reason choose him to speak briefly to this somewhat difficult point:

Lex ergo dei immaculata caritas est, que non quod sibi utile est querit, sed quod multis. Lex autem domini dicitur, sive quod ipse ex ea vivat, sive quod eam nullus nisi eius dono possideat. Nec absurdum videatur quod dixi etiam deum vivere ex lege, cum non alia quam caritate dixerim. Quid vero in summa et beata illa trinitate summam et ineffabilem illam conservat unitatem nisi caritas? Lex est ergo et lex domini caritas, que trinitatem in unitate quodammodo cohibet et colliget in vinculo pacis. Nec tamen me estimet caritatem hic accipere qualitatem vel aliquod accidens (alioquin in deo dicerim—quod absit—esse aliquid quod deus non est) sed substantiam illam divinam quod utique nec novum nec insolitum est, dicente Johanne, Deus caritas est. *Dicitur ergo recte caritas et deum et dei donum. Itaque caritas dat caritatem, substantiva accidentalem. Ubi dantem significat, substantia est; ubi donum qualitas. Hec est lex eterna, creatrix et gubernatrix universitatis.*

Immaculate charity, therefore, is the law of God, which seeks not what is useful to itself but what is useful to many. For it is said to be the law of God either because He lives by it or because no one possesses it if not as a gift of Him. Nor should it seem absurd that I said that even God lives by law, since I should have said by none other than charity. What indeed in that supreme and blessed Trinity conserves the supreme and ineffable oneness if not charity? Charity therefore is the law and the law of God which somehow holds the Trinity in unity and binds it in the bond of peace. However, let it not be thought that I take charity in that case as a quality or as something accidental (else

I should be saying—which God forbid—that there is in God something which is not God); but I take it as that divine substance, which is in no way either new or unusual, as John says: *Deus caritas est.* Charity is therefore rightly said to be God and the gift of God. And thus charity gives charity, the substantial gives the accidental. Where it means the giver, it is the substance; where the gift, the accident. This is the eternal law, the creator and the governor of all things.

*

* *

It was inevitable that between two such divergent conceptions of love as troubadour love of woman and Christian love of God conflict should arise: inevitable because in his "philosophy" the troubadour found no place for Christian love as such. Neither did Christian love make any room at all for troubadour love. The antagonism of the two may be put in its simplest formulation by saying that within troubadour ideology there is no place for an object of love higher than the lady; whereas in the Christian, not only can there be no object of love higher than God but all other loves must show subordination to love of Him. The trouble was precisely that the troubadour could always forget to acknowledge that subordination. For his love of *domina* was without reference to God.

If this is a conflict, it is of course a very one-sided affair, since, after all, the troubadour was a Christian but the Christian lover of God was not a troubadour. For no one of the poets writing in the troubadour tradition, whatever his time or country, would ever have denied the truth of what good love or charity is and what bad love or lust is as Augustine had expressed it, for instance, in his treatise *On Christian Doctrine:*

I mean by charity that affection of the mind which aims at the enjoyment of God for His own sake, and the enjoyment of one's self and one's neighbor in subordination to God; by lust I mean that affection of the mind which aims at enjoying one's self and one's neighbor and other corporeal things without reference to God.

Nor would any one of these lovers of women have found anything but the simple truth in the little picture which Augustine gives in that same treatise of our mortal state in this life, or in his definition of the radical difference between using and enjoying:

For to enjoy a thing is to rest with satisfaction in it for its own sake. To use, on the other hand, is to employ whatever means are at one's disposal to obtain what one desires, if it is a proper object of desire; for an unlawful use ought rather to be called an abuse. Suppose, then, we were wanderers in a strange country, and could not live happily away from our fatherland, and that we felt wretched in our wanderings, and wishing to put an end to our misery, determined to return home. We find, however, that we must make use of some mode of conveyance, either by land or water, in order to reach that fatherland where our enjoyment is to commence. But the beauty of the country through which we pass, and the very pleasure of the motion, charm our hearts, and turning these things which we ought to use into objects of enjoyment, we become unwilling to hasten the end of our journey, and becoming engrossed in a factitious delight, our thoughts are diverted from that home whose delights would make us truly happy. Such is a picture of our condition in this life of mortality. We have wandered far from God; and if we wish to return to our Father's home, this world must be used, not enjoyed, so that the invisible things of God may be clearly seen, being understood by the things that are made [Romans I, 20]— that is, that by means of what is material and temporary we may lay hold upon that which is spiritual and eternal.

No, none of the poets would have denied this truth. Only the trouble was that the ideology of the love they celebrated demanded that the lady be as *domina*—which is feminine for *master*. And as master, she was to be exalted as it was fitting that a lover and a servant's song should exalt her: to a point beyond which there is no one higher. It was also to the greater glory of the God of Love that *domina* should be extolled; for this, the God would no doubt cause reward to be made to his faithful servant. The result could not have been other than it was: this love of woman which the poets sang was necessarily without subordination to God. Seen in the frame of Augustine's little picture, it was indeed a straying from the path which could lead to the peace of Heaven. It was a byway through beautiful country, off to one side of the main road, and in order to follow it the poet must for a while play truant. If only for a little while, he must manage to close his ears to the stern voice of moral reason. In the end there would be time to heed that voice and to repent of the truancy. Meanwhile there might be songs and poetry; meanwhile a God of Love and *domina,* if only for a time, might rule over this little world. Finally, then, the truth could, of course, be acknowledged: all this had been wrong. This was bad love. Within the larger frame of Christian love, this love of woman had to be recanted.

Recantation even became a part of the tradition. There is no better example of this inevitable final turning from love of woman to love of God than what a famous "theologian" of courtly love wrote toward the end of his *Art of Love.* In the first two books of his work, Andreas Cappellanus gives a most detailed course of instruction in that art to a young friend named Walter (and what an amazing course it is!). But then comes the time, at the beginning of the third book, when he feels that he must admonish his pupil as follows:

Now, friend Walter, if you will lend attentive ears to those things which after careful consideration we wrote down for you because you urged us so strongly, you can lack nothing in the art of love, since in this little book we gave you the theory of the subject, fully and completely, being willing to accede to your requests because of the great love we have for you. You should know that we did not do this because we consider it advisable for you or any other man to fall in love, but for fear lest you might think us stupid; we believe though that any man who devotes his efforts to love loses all his usefulness. Read this little book, then, not as one seeking to take up the life of a lover, but that, invigorated by the theory and trained to excite the minds of women to love, you may, by refraining from so doing, win an eternal recompense and thereby deserve a greater reward from God. For God is more pleased with a man who is able to sin and does not than with a man who has no opportunity to sin.

Then again, at the end of the whole work, the Chaplain's final words to his young friend are these:

Be mindful, therefore, Walter, to have your lamps always supplied, that is, have the supplies of charity and good works. Be mindful ever to watch, lest the unexpected coming of the Bridegroom find you asleep in sins. Avoid then, Walter, practicing the mandates of love, and labor in constant watchfulness so that when the Bridegroom cometh, He may find you wakeful; do not let worldly delight make you lie down in your sins, trusting to the youth of your body and confident that the Bridegroom will be late, since as He tells us Himself, we know neither the day nor the hour.

Galahad and the Grail had broken in upon the romance of Lancelot as yet another manifestation of this same spirit of recantation. Like the coming of the Bridegroom was their coming to the world of courtly love. And there were yet other ways of crying *mea culpa.* At least one third of the troubadours in the south of France are reported to have turned to the cloister and to God in their last years—and it does not much matter if this be only legend. The substantial pattern of the matter is still there, even in the rumor. We find it in Chaucer and in Gower and in Juan Ruiz in Spain. In one form or another repentance did come to be a part of the tradition of courtly love.

Petrarch is the last troubadour and he presents no exception in this. The arrangement of the poems in his *Canzoniere* is his own; and the last poem is beyond any mistake this recantation. Only Petrarch took the matter a step farther. He began with repentance. The first poem of the *Canzoniere* sings a theme of *vanitas.* And then throughout the three hundred and sixty-six poems (at moments artfully spaced), he turns from Laura to God. Thus, in the eleventh year of his love for her, he writes his famous sonnet-prayer beginning,

> *Padre del ciel, dopo i perduti giorni*
> *dopo le notti vaneggiando spese . . .*
>
> Father in heaven, after the lost days,
> after the nights spent raving . . .

Petrarch knows very well why this love of his for Laura must be renounced. In his *Secretum,* a dialogue in Latin prose, he arranges for no less an authority than St. Augustine to tell him clearly why:

She [says the Saint, speaking of Laura] turned your mind from heavenly things and your desire from the Creator to the creature.

But Petrarch shows himself to be no docile catechumen, even at the feet of such a master. In fact, he makes a spirited defense of his love for Laura, voicing exactly what had long since become one of the central doctrines of courtly love: namely, that love is the source of all virtue and all good. As he faces Augustine's accusing finger in the third day of this dialogue, we hear the poet deny that his love for Laura can be bad love:

I can only say that whatever I am I owe to her. And if I have any portion of fame or glory, I should never have attained it had she not cultivated with her very noble affections the little seed of virtue which nature had planted in my breast. She recalled my youthful mind from all unworthy things and . . . forced it to look on lofty things. . . What other desire did I have in youth if not to please her alone who had so pleased me? And in order to do this you know to what labors I yoked myself, scorning a thousand lascivious and voluptuous things. And now you wish me to forget or to love more moderately her who lifted me from the company of the vulgar herd, who was my guide in all my ways, who spurred my tardy talent and awoke my sleepy mind.

Lancelot, though he was no poet, might at one time have claimed much the same for his love of Guinevere. This is *amor-virtù, hohe Minne.* Even Platonic love seems closer to the flesh than this.

But the important fact to see is that distance from the flesh makes no difference. For all that, this love stands condemned and for the reason that Augustine has given. There is no escape. Petrarch will have to end his *Canzoniere* with a song of repentance; he must still turn from Laura to the Virgin and to God:

Vergine, quante lacrime ho già sparte,
quante lusinghe e quanti preghi indarno,
pur per mia pena e per mio grave danno!
Da poi ch'i'nacqui in su la riva d'Arno,
cercando or questa et or quell'altra parte,
non è stata mia vita altro ch'affanno.
Mortal bellezza, atti e parole m'hanno
tutta ingombrata l'alma.
Vergine sacra et alma,
non tardar, ch'i'son forse all'ultimo anno.

Virgin, how many tears have I already shed, how many blandishments and entreaties in vain, even for my own suffering and grave harm to myself! From the time I was born on the bank of the Arno, seeking now here, now elsewhere, my life has been only woe. Mortal beauty, actions and words have completely burdened my soul. Holy and blessed Virgin, do not delay, for I may be in my last year.

This final prayer is much longer than this. Its last word is *pace*. It is indeed a prayer for peace. But peace is what above all else is absent from the world of courtly love. By the very nature of this love, it was not possible that the lover should ever know peace in it—not without bringing love to an end. Any supreme reward from his lady which might bring peace would, if granted, mean the end of virtuous love and of his inspiration as a poet. Moreover, as clearly stated by Christian doctrine itself, the place of that true beatitude which is our final place of rest is not in any creature. It is in God, even as St. Thomas explains in his *Summa theologica*:

It is not possible for any created good to constitute man's happiness. For happiness is the perfect good which lulls the appetite altogether; else it would not be the last end, if something yet remained to be desired. Now the object of the will, i.e., of man's appetite, is the universal good. . . Hence it is evident that nought can lull man's will save the universal good. This is to be found not in any creature but in God alone, because every creature has goodness by participation.

Not that the poet had not looked toward Heaven in his love of woman. He had indeed always looked upward and for the reason that his lady was always above him. Courtly love is never a love of equals. *Domina* is always above the poet and seems, as the tradition grows older, increasingly higher and higher above, until finally she begins to resemble an angel. Being always higher, she ought always to lead to higher things. And she did, as we have heard Petrarch maintain as he faced Augustine. But *domina* she must remain; and as *domina* she must be the last and only object of desire in her poet-lover's upward gaze. How might he dare look beyond her? The little closed world of this kind of love did not allow for such irreverence. Yet, as every troubadour knew, beyond and further up was God.

*

*   *

Our time as readers of the *Vita Nuova* is not wasted if we stay long enough with this matter to understand that the so-called *donna angelicata,* the lady-made-angel, of the lyric poetry being written before and in Dante's time in Italy did not bring in herself the solution to the conflict between troubadour love and Christian love, as some historians of literature would seem to suggest. These, on the authority of Dante, usually speak of Guido Guinicelli of Bologna as the father of a school of poets called the *dolce stil nuovo;* and since they find the lady-made-angel in Guinicelli's poems, they appear to give to the Bolognese poet the credit for being the first to point the way out of the conflict. The picture which these histories give is, at any rate, a hazy one; those which do intend that the credit for the solution should go to Guinicelli think to find the grounds for this in his famous song, "Love and the Gentle Heart."

We shall here recall only the last two stanzas of this *canzone,* these being that part where the solution, if it is there at all, would be found.

The first of these stanzas presents a simile which may be paraphrased in this way: Even as God shines from his Heaven upon an Angelic Intelligence, more brightly than the sun to mortal eyes; and the Intelligence, looking up to God, turns its appointed sphere of Heaven and realizes the idea and the will of God below; so it is with the lady and her lover. For the lover looks up to her as the Intelligence does to God, and by the light which comes from his lady, he accomplishes his good work in the world (that is, his art).

This, obviously, is *amor-virtù* again, the kind that Petrarch rushed in to defend so warmly before Augustine.

But in the final stanza of the poem, God himself is seen to protest this simile. We are shown a little scene before the judgment seat of God. The poet imagines that his soul stands facing God and that God, having reference to the simile in the foregoing stanza of this poem, will say to him,

What presumption is this on your part? You have passed beyond the heavens and come even up to me in a simile of vain love. But to *me* belongs the praise and to the Queen of Heaven.

But the poet, we learn, will be ready with his answer to God. He will reply (and the poem ends with these words):

She had the appearance of an angel who came from Your kingdom. No sin is imputable to me if I loved her.

But can we accept this as a sufficient reply to God? Is this any solution? In short, is the poet right or is God right?

Should we not rather observe that Guinicelli has deliberately ended his poem with an ambiguity? He has refused at the end to take sides. The very point, the conceit, of his poem is to present the conflict without solution.

It is a "philosophical" *canzone* and was apparently much respected by Dante and the other Florentine poets of his generation.

To that same generation of poets, Guinicelli in his lyrics bequeathed two themes for poems of love. These amount to two focuses for poems. In one of them the poet looks at the object of love, at the lady, and sings her praises. He sees her approach in all her angelic beauty. She seems a miracle upon earth. Here is an example of the handling of the theme in Guinicelli:

> *I'vo' del ver la mia donna laudare*
> *ed assembrargli la rosa e lo giglio;*
> *più che la stella diana splende e pare,*
> *e ciò ch'è lassù bello a lei somiglio.*
> *Verde rivera a lei rassembro e l'aire,*
> *tutti color di fior, giallo e vermiglio,*
> *oro e azzurro e ricche gioi' per dare;*
> *medesmo Amor per lei raffina meglio.*
> *Passa per via adorna e sì gentile*
> *ch'abbassa orgoglio a cui dona salute,*
> *e fa'l di nostra fè, se non la crede,*
> *e non si pò appressar omo ch'è vile;*
> *ancor vi dico c'ha maggior vertute:*
> *null'om pò mal pensar fin che la vede.*

I wish to praise my lady truly and compare the rose and the lily to her; more than the morning star does she shine and appear; and all that is beautiful on high I liken to her. She is like a green shore, I say, like the air, like all colors of flowers, yellow and vermilion, gold and azure, like rich jewels meant for gifts. Through her love itself becomes finer. She passes along the way so fair and so gentle that she lays pride low in him to whom she gives her greeting, and she converts him to our faith if he is an unbeliever, and no man who is base may approach; she has, I tell you, an even greater virtue: no one can think ill as long as he sees her.

The other theme turns to consider the subject of love. Its focus is on the poet and on the effects on him of love for such a creature as this. It finds him to be overcome by the miracle of her being, blinded by the radiance that shines about her. Almost the whole corpus of *dolce stil nuovo* poetry is made up of variations on these two themes. Here, on the one hand, is the lady who is a miracle. And here, on the other, is the poet wounded to death by love, fainting in her presence, unable to tolerate the brightness of such a creature. So great is her *virtù* that it deprives him of his. She is as a bolt of lightning. If the lightning does not kill her all too mortal lover, it leaves him calling for death.

Here again is an example from Guinicelli:

> *Lo vostro bel saluto e'l gentil sguardo*
> *che fate quando v'encontro m'ancide;*
> *Amor m'assale e già non ha reguardo*
> *s'elli face peccato o ver mercide,*
> *che per mezzo lo cor me lancia un dardo*
> *ched oltre in parti lo taglia e divide;*
> *parlar non posso che'n gran pene eo ardo*
> *sì come quello che sua morte vide.*
> *Per li occhi passa come fa lo trono,*
> *che fer per la finestra de la torre*
> *e ciò che dentro trova spezza e fende;*
> *remagno come statua d'ottono*
> *ove vita nè spirto non ricorre,*
> *se non che la figura d'omo rende.*

Your fine greeting and the gentle glance that you give when I meet you kills me; Love assails me and is quite unconcerned whether he give offense or favor, because he casts a dart through my heart which cleaves it through and divides it into parts; I cannot speak for I burn in great pain as one who sees his death. It passes through the eyes as does the bolt which strikes through the window of the tower and what it finds inside it breaks and splits. I remain as a statue of brass, in which neither life nor spirit dwells, except that it gives the appearance of a man.

Here now is one of several poems on this same theme which may
be found among the works of Guido Cavalcanti, Dante's "first
friend":

> L'anima mia vilment'è sbigottita
> della battaglia ch'ell'have dal core;
> che s'ella sente pur un poco Amore
> più presso a lui che non sole, la more.
> Sta come quella che non ha valore,
> ch'è per temenza da lo cor partita:
> e chi vedesse com'ella è fuggita
> diria per certo: questi non ha vita.
>   Per li occhi venne la battaglia in pria
> che ruppe ogni valore immantenente,
> sì che del colpo fu strutta la mente.
> Qualunque è quei che più allegrezza sente,
> se vedesse li spirti fuggir via,
> di grande sua pietate piangeria.

My soul is basely dismayed at the battle it has with my heart, for if
it feels that Love is even a little nearer than usual to it [the heart], it dies.
It is as one without strength, who through fear has departed from the
heart; and whoever would see how it has fled would surely say: this
man is without life. The attack came first through the eyes and broke
all strength immediately, so that the mind was destroyed by the blow.
Whoever is he who feels most happiness, if he saw my spirits flee, would
weep out of great pity.

This, as any attentive reader will recall, is the theme of more
than one poem in the *Vita Nuova* itself. There are, in fact, several
examples in sonnets which come before the God of Love has dis-
appeared; as, for instance, the poem of chapter xiv inspired by that
most painful time when Beatrice joined with the other ladies in
ridicule (*gabbo*) of this lover who could not so much as endure the
presence of his beloved.

> Con l'altre donne mia vista gabbate,
> e non pensate, donna, onde si mova
> ch'io vi rassembri sì figura nova
> quando riguardo la vostra beltate.
> Se lo saveste, non poria Pietate

tener più contra me l'usata prova,
che Amor, quando sì presso a voi mi trova,
prende baldanza e tanta securtate,
* che fere tra'miei spiriti paurosi,*
e quale ancide, e qual pinge di fore,
sì che solo remane a veder vui:
ond'io mi cangio in figura d'altrui,
ma non sì ch'io non senta bene allore
li guai de li scacciati tormentosi.

Along with other ladies you make sport at me, and you do not think, my lady, whence it comes that I become so strange a figure before you when I look upon your beauty. If you but knew, Pity could no longer hold out against me as is her wont. For Love, when he finds me near you, takes courage and such assurance that he strikes out among my frightened spirits, and some he slays and some he drives away, so that he alone stays to see you: wherefore I am changed into another's form, but not so much that I do not then hear very well the wails of those who are tortured at being driven out.

It is an old theme like that of the moth and the flame. If this is "bad" love, it is bad now only in so far as it threatens the lover with death. It is still troubadour love and still *amor-virtù*, and is only a development *à outrance* of the accepted doctrine. Moreover, one readily observes that each of these themes is the natural complement of the other. Either might have arisen out of the other. Indeed, both, in a sense, are but a single theme in praise of the lady. It is to her greater glory that in her presence her lover is "blasted with ecstasy"—and to the greater glory of the God of Love.

But Guido Cavalcanti became philosophical about the matter. He undertook to theorize seriously about this power of love to undo the lover. Tradition has it that it was Guido Orlandi who wrote to Cavalcanti asking him many questions of Love, among them the question whether "Love was life or death." "From Love's power death often comes," Cavalcanti replied in his famous (and famously obscure) song beginning *Donna me prega* (A lady begs me), and became the theorist of a love which is dark and tragic.

Now Dante, like all the other poets about him, had tried his own hand at the two themes, and we have seen how some of the poems found their way into the *Vita Nuova*. But the point of greatest importance for our grasp of the significance of the *Vita Nuova* is that Dante did not terminate the upward way of love at a point where the lover succumbed to the power of love. The way of love as he saw it was at first, to be sure, a most painful one. But to Guido Orlandi's question, "Is love life or death?" Dante's reply is that it is life, that love for Beatrice, at any rate, is life. Dante, as we shall see better later, found a way out of the tragic love of his first friend. He also found a way to go beyond the conflict of love of woman with love of God, bringing to the thesis and the antithesis of the one and the other that synthesis which managed to reject neither the one nor the other but to keep both in a single suspension—in a single theory of love. The *Vita Nuova* is that theory. It is *theory* in a first sense of the word: a *beholding* of how certain things may be.

*

*   *

In that long conflict between two conceptions of love, troubadour and Christian, the *Vita Nuova* has a public context which gives special meaning to all its parts and to the pattern of its action. That action begins with troubadour love. But long before it ends, at a point, in fact, near its middle, it has arrived at the other kind of love. Thus, only by seeing the *Vita Nuova* against the background of a tradition in which recantation was the only way which the poet of love of woman had found of turning at the end and embracing Christian love (as in the end he must), can we see the uniqueness of the solution which Dante has brought to the problem and something of the tension which in such a context any solution would have.

The disappearance of the God of Love from the *Vita Nuova* is nothing less than a deliberate removal. That removal, however, is all in the way of recantation of troubadour love which the *Vita Nuova* makes. The God of Love is, indeed, the veriest sign and symbol of such love. But if this is recantation, it is very unlike the traditional kind, because even if the God is abolished, love of woman is not abandoned. Beatrice remains. In fact, the whole authority of Love is transferred to her. Beatrice is Love. And Beatrice remains to the end. Yet, between love of her and love of God there is no conflict. When the *Vita Nuova* ends, it faces God; but it keeps Beatrice. How can it do this without the usual palinode?

The twenty-fourth and twenty-fifth chapters of the book do much to provide the answer, although those chapters are actually but parts of a whole strategy working toward this goal: that, to the very end, love of woman may be kept in love of God.

The particular role of those two chapters in bringing this about must now be clear. They belong to the unfolding of the metaphor of the Book of Memory, to a process of gradual revelation made possible through a multiple gloss. The revelation is this: that love of Beatrice is something too large to be contained within the ideology of troubadour love. Love of Beatrice reaches far beyond the powers of a God of Love. That was not clear at first. But that is the way of revelation. One after another, however, the glosses of the Book of Memory disclose that Beatrice is a miracle, that love of her is a love whose other name is charity, being also love of God. For it is charity that bursts the narrow confines of troubadour love. It is the presence of charity, hidden in the beginning, which demands at a midpoint on the way of progression from love to charity that the God of Love be abolished. There is no room and no authority for a troubadour God of Love in the universe of Christian love. That universe is ruled by charity, and the only God who may inhabit it is a jealous God who is Himself charity. *Deus caritas est.*

The definition of love in chapter xxv in terms of *substance* and *accident* does not in itself express all this. But it allows for this to become so. According to philosophers of great authority in Dante's time all passions are accidents. Love, of course, is a passion in any philosophy. Since the individual human being is a substance, love must be an "accident in a substance." Hence, this definition of love as an accident in a substance appears to say only that love is a passion occurring in individuals. There is nothing in the definition which says that love is charity. And yet, when in other parts of this book it is gradually revealed that love of Beatrice is charity, the strategic importance of this definition is that it has allowed for and does not gainsay a love which is revealed to be charity. That is, the definition not only serves to look back and deny a troubadour

God of Love. It also looks forward and makes provision for what is to come: namely, for the revelation that Beatrice is love and that the love she is is charity.

We know from St. Bernard that charity, on the one hand, is to be distinguished as *substantial* charity, which is alone in God; and, on the other, as *created* charity, which is all in the way of love that the creature can experience. Thus love in God is "substance." But on earth and in this life and in human beings it is "accident" because it cannot exist to itself, but is only a participation in substantial charity.

The poet's gloss has allowed for all this, and all this means simply the Christian truth. His definition denies that the figure of a God of Love can be the truth about love. The truth is that love is not, as it might appear to be by such a personification, a substance on this earth.

But this definition must avoid obstructing a positive truth: the revelation that henceforth, "to anyone who will look subtly at the matter," Beatrice is Love—metaphorically, of course, since it was in a sense by metaphor, too, that the God of Love was Love. But the God of Love was no creature. He was a God, and to deny that love is a substance is to deny him. Beatrice is no god. Whether she be seen as a mortal woman or as a miracle (and she is both), Beatrice is a creature. Thus the definition, denying love as a substance, looks ahead to what is to be revealed about Beatrice and about love of her: namely, that she is love and that the love she is is charity. For the love which comes to us on earth is, as St. Bernard has told us, created love. Of created love a *God* of Love may not be a sign; but Beatrice, who is a creature, may.

We know from both St. Augustine and St. Bernard, moreover, that love is a gift of God. Now the Book of Memory reveals nothing more clearly than that Beatrice is a gift of God. She comes from Heaven, a bearer of beatitude. Between God and her lover she is the medium by which a love which begins in Heaven can reach down to him on earth. And, through her death and her return to Heaven, she is also the means by which the love of her lover is led back to God. The course of love is therefore like a circle, descending from God and ascending up to God—through Beatrice.

The name for such a love as this, coming from God and returning to God, is truly charity. And Beatrice's other name is love.

This scheme by which Beatrice holds a medial position, not only in the downward path of love from God to a man but in the upward and returning path of love from man to God as well, is the solution which Dante has brought to the conflict between love of woman and love of God. Love of Beatrice is charity, which means that love of her begins in God and ends in God. This love's upward way does not come to a stop at *domina* as did the love of the troubadours. It goes beyond to God, whence it came. It is, in short, a love which can only be if a miracle can be; can be only if the supernatural break through the shell of the natural and a gift of God which is charity appear on earth. It is such love as can be only if a *Beatrice* can be.

Thus, to an eye alert to the public context of the *Vita Nuova,* what is most remarkable about it is the way in which, as a theory of *good* love, it has kept love of woman to the very end—to the final sentence of the book, in fact:

E poi piaccia a colui che è sire de la cortesia che la mia anima se ne possa gire a vedere la gloria de la sua donna cioè di quella benedetta Beatrice la quale gloriosamente mira ne la faccia di colui qui est per omnia secula benedictus.

And then may it please Him who is the lord of courtesy that my soul may depart to behold the glory of its lady, that is, of that blessed Beatrice who in glory gazes upon the face of Him who is blessed forever and ever.

Between the lover and God, Beatrice (as the *Vita Nuova* has it) remains. A troubadour's love would have seen only Beatrice, a saint's love would have sought only God. But the last sentence of the *Vita Nuova* is the affirmation of a pattern which one who was not a saint, but who refused to remain a troubadour, saw as the final expression of a love which began where the troubadours began and ended with the saints. It is the final aspiration of Beatrice's lover that he may one day see her who in her turn sees God.

IV

Vita Nuova

THE three visions foretelling the death of Beatrice all bear the mark of a number *nine* and point thus to special meaning in that number. They would seem also, by being *three,* to stress the presence of some special meaning for the root of nine as well. The poet's gloss on the death of Beatrice and on the number nine (chapter xxix) does much to confirm this: three is the "factor" by itself of nine, three is the sign of the "factor" of miracles which is the Holy Trinity.

Furthermore, it is precisely in terms of a number three that the center of the *Vita Nuova* may be located. The middle of the work is plainly marked by that second of three *canzoni,* the poem in which the death of Beatrice (her unreal death) shows a certain resemblance to the death of Christ.

Nor is this all in the way of a symmetrical arrangement of the poems to be noted in the Book of Memory. In all there are thirty-one poems in the *Vita Nuova.* Here again must not an eye alert to the meanings concealed in numbers see the sign of the Trinity which is Three and One?

Moreover, in contrast with the three *canzoni,* all of the other poems in the book are shorter poems, minor forms or fragments: most are sonnets, but there are *three* exceptions: one ballata, one stanza of an unfinished *canzone,* and another poem made up of two stanzas only of a *canzone.* Among such as these, therefore, the three longer poems can have prominence by length alone and can be used as markers to divide the others into groups. That they are used as such becomes evident with the first *canzone,* for that poem is explicitly said to mark the end of the poet's first subject matter and the beginning of his second. This *canzone* thus leaves behind itself a certain number of shorter poems which thereby become a group to themselves. One notices, too, that these poems are ten in number and that all but one are sonnets.

Such clear signs of a deliberate design at the beginning can well prompt us to look to the end. There we are not surprised, I imagine, by what we discover: the end balances exactly the beginning; the last *canzone* is followed by ten poems just as the first is preceded by ten; and in this final group the poems are all sonnets but one. Hence, the first and the third of the three *canzoni* stand at equal distance respectively from beginning and end, marking off the shorter poems into a first group and a third.

What of the center? There the pattern is clearly confirmed. For between the first and the third *canzoni* there are nine poems. And, in this group of nine, the poem which is at the exact center is the second of the three *canzoni,* which thus becomes necessarily the central poem in respect to a number nine as well as to a number three.

It is all undeniably part of a conscious design in the arrangement of the poems of the *Vita Nuova,* amounting to a sort of external architecture, a kind of façade which, for all its evidence, appears to have escaped the notice of readers of the book until around the middle of the last century. It had, at any rate, to be rediscovered then. By now, the introductions to most editions of the *Vita Nuova* make a point of it, usually seeing the whole design as one to be represented by the figures 10; I; 4-II-4; III; 10 (Roman numerals being the *canzoni*). But, given the exceptional importance of the number nine in this work, it would seem much more significant to consider the first and last groups of the shorter poems as made up of nine plus one. This would require only that we count the first poem of the *Vita Nuova* as an introductory one, much as we count the first canto of *Inferno*; and that we consider the last poem of the book as a kind of epilogue which, given its nature, it may well be. Such a pattern seems more meaningful for the *Vita Nuova* in that it can be stated in terms of nine and three and one: 1, 9; I; 4-II-4; III; 9, 1. Or more simply, and with perhaps even greater suggestiveness, as 1;9;1;9;1;9;1, since in this way the mysterious number nine is more clearly seen to occur three times.

This is more than a matter of extrinsic ornament. Here on the surface are ripples and eddies which are all so many signs of what we know already to lie deeper in the current of the action. As such signs, they make their own contribution to what is the principal intention of the whole form of the Book of Memory: the revealing through signs that Beatrice is a miracle, that she is herself a number nine which, like miracles, is the product of three times three.

By looking intently at such a miraculous object of love, we were able to trace a line of progression from love to charity. Now, if we begin once more at these surface signs of miracle and proceed to sound the deeper currents of the action, we shall see, by keeping our eyes this time on the subject of love, that there is yet another line of progression to be followed out. It too, like the other, is a line reaching upward. The subject of love is no miracle. The subject of love is the poet. The Book of Memory is his, his is the new life in love.

The progression which we must now follow out is that of this new life itself. In it, we may note at once, the number three is revealed again. For before the end is reached, the poet has found three subject matters for his poems. And these subject matters, marked off as three even in the surface design, are revealed, in their turn, to be stages in the new life, three stages.

In this manuscript Book of Memory the poems are, after all, the primary text; the rest is either a gloss to the poems or a gloss on that gloss. Hence, if there are three stages in the poet's love, that fact ought to be visible first in the poems. And so it is, although were there no gloss in prose to point out that fact, we might easily fail to see it.

But it is much easier to see that there are three subject matters for the poems than it is to give them names. The "gloss" in the Book of Memory does not tell specifically what their names might be. It makes, however, a rather clear suggestion of them. For instance, in the prose of chapter XVII we are told that when the poet had finished the last three of the first group of poems, he felt that these had been the "narrators" of all that he needed to say of his own "state" in love; and that the time, therefore, had come for him to find a new subject matter for his poems so that, as the Book of Memory has recorded it, the change comes first in respect to the poems. And this is as near as the prose ever comes to supplying a name for what has been the first subject matter of the poems: it is, we see, the state of the poet.

But do we expect lyric poems to be about anything else? Does a lyric poet actually ever write about anything other than his own inner state?

It would seem that he does, and the following chapter tells us as much. For something happened, something which made the poet realize that his poems must be no longer about himself. It takes the whole of that chapter XVIII to tell the "reason" of this, a chapter containing no poem of its own, but presenting what is surely one of the most charming episodes of the whole story:

Con ciò sia cosa che per la vista mia molte persone avessero compreso lo secreto del mio cuore, certe donne, le quali adunate s'erano dilettandosi l'una ne la compagnia de l'altra, sapeano bene lo mio cuore, però che ciascuna di loro era stata a molte mie sconfitte; e io passando appresso di loro, sì come da la fortuna menato, fui chiamato da una di queste gentili donne. La donna che m'avea chiamato era donna di molto leggiadro parlare; sì che quand'io fui giunto dinanzi da loro, e vidi bene che la mia gentilissima donna non era con esse, rassicurandomi le salutai, e domandai che piacesse loro. Le donne erano molte, tra le quali n'avea certe che si rideano tra loro; altre v'erano che mi guardavano aspettando che io dovessi dire; altre v'erano che parlavano tra loro. De le quali una, volgendo li suoi occhi verso me e chiamandomi per nome, disse queste parole: "A che fine ami tu questa tua donna, poi che tu non puoi sostenere la sua presenza? Dilloci, chè certo lo fine di cotale amore conviene che sia novissimo." E poi che m'ebbe dette queste parole, non solamente ella, ma tutte l'altre cominciaro ad attendere in vista la mia risponsione. Allora dissi queste parole loro: "Madonne, lo fine del mio amore fue già lo saluto di questa donna, forse di cui voi intendete, e in quello dimorava la beatitudine, chè era fine di tutti li miei desiderii. Ma poi che le piacque di negarlo a me, lo mio segnore Amore, la sua merzede, ha posto tutta la mia beatitudine in quello che non mi puote venire meno." Allora queste donne cominciaro a parlare tra loro; e sì come talora vedemo cadere l'acqua mischiata di bella neve, così mi parea udire le loro parole uscire mischiate di sospiri. E poi che alquanto ebbero parlato tra loro, anche mi disse questa donna che m'avea prima parlato, queste parole: "Noi ti preghiamo che tu ne dichi ove sta questa tua beatitudine." Ed io, rispondendo lei, dissi cotanto: "In quelle parole che lodano la donna mia." Allora mi rispuose questa che mi parlava: "Se tu ne dicessi vero, quelle parole che tu n'hai dette in notificando la tua condizione, avrestù operate con altro intendimento." Onde io, pensando a queste parole, quasi vergognoso mi partio da loro, e venia dicendo fra me medesimo: "Poi che è tanta beatitudine in quelle parole che lodano la mia donna, perchè altro parlare è stato lo mio?" E però propuosi di prendere per matera de lo mio parlare sempre mai quello che fosse loda di questa gentilissima; e pensando molto a ciò pareami avere impresa troppo alta matera quanto a me, sì che non ardia di cominciare; e così dimorai alquanti dì con disiderio di dire e con paura di cominciare.

Inasmuch as from my aspect many persons had understood my heart's secret, certain ladies, who had come together, finding pleasure in each other's company, knew my heart very well, since every one of them had been present at many of my defeats; and I, passing near them as one led by fortune, was called by one of these gentle ladies. The lady who had called me was a lady of very gracious speech; so that when I was come before them and saw well that my most gentle lady was not with them, reassuring myself I greeted them and asked them what might be their pleasure. The ladies were many, among whom were some who were laughing among themselves. Others there were who were watching me, expecting me to speak. There were others who spoke among themselves. Of these one, turning her eyes toward me and calling me by name, spoke these words: "To what end do you love this your lady, since you cannot endure her presence? Tell us this, for certainly the end of such a love must be most strange." And when she had spoken these words to me, not only she but all the others began visibly to await my reply. Then I said these words to them: "My ladies, the end of my love was once the greeting of this lady, whom perchance you have in mind, and in that dwelt beatitude, for it was the end of all my desires. But when it pleased her to deny it to me, my lord Love, through his grace, put all my beatitude in that which cannot fail me." Then these ladies began to speak among themselves; and as sometimes we see rain fall mingled with beautiful snow, so it seemed to me to hear their words issue mingled with sighs. And when they had spoken among themselves a while, that same lady who had first spoken to me said these words to me: "We pray you that you tell us wherein resides this your beatitude." And I, replying to her, said thus: "In those words which praise my lady." Then she who was speaking to me replied to me: "If you were telling us the truth, those words which you spoke to us in setting forth your condition you would have used with another intention." Whereupon, thinking on these words, I left them as one ashamed, and came away saying to myself: "Since there is so much beatitude in those words which praise my lady, why have my words been of anything else?" And therefore I proposed henceforth to take as the subject of my words whatever might be in praise of this most gentle lady; and thinking much on this, it seemed to me that I had undertaken too lofty a subject for me, so that I did not dare to begin; and thus I remained some days desiring to write and afraid to begin.

This then, is the "reason" for the first *canzone,* for its subject matter, and for the second group of poems in the *Vita Nuova* which follows it. And this is, at the same time, also the reason for bringing the first group of poems to an end. The poet had come to see that he ought to write no more poems about himself. That subject, he felt, was exhausted. From now on he would write only in praise of his lady. It is a change in inspiration, the discovery of a new *direction* for his attention as poet. No longer will the eye of the poet focus upon himself and the effects of love on him. It will now turn to "madónna" and sing in praise of her and of her alone.

We know that, beginning especially with Guinicelli, two themes became predominant in the Italian love lyric, and we have seen what these were. Dante, like the others, had used them in poems. Now, in view of what we shall see to be the particular grouping of the poems according to subject in the *Vita Nuova,* we shall hardly fail to wonder if those same two themes have not become precisely the first two "subject matters" of the book. If they have, then we ought to observe that the *Vita Nuova* was, for one thing, a way of using poems probably already written on established themes before it was conceived as a whole made up of poems and prose.

The possibility of those two themes being the first two "subjects" of the poems in the *Vita Nuova* can at least serve to sharpen our view of what the first two subjects of the poems are. The two themes in the tradition were of the nature of two focuses, as we have seen. One theme turned the light of attention on the poet and the state of the poet, finding him done almost to death by the miraculous *virtù* of the object of love. Now is this theme not exactly the subject of the first group of poems in the *Vita Nuova?* We see that it is, and most clearly in the last three of those ten poems. The first of these is that sonnet written on the occasion of the wedding feast where, when Beatrice had walked into the room, the poet (as he afterwards told the friend who took him there) had suddenly stood on the verge of death. And the other two of the three poems are also on this same theme: the threat of death to the lover. The second is fairly representative of all three:

> *Ciò che m'incontra, ne la mente more,*
> *quand'i' vegno a veder voi, bella gioia;*
> *e quand'io vi son presso, i'sento Amore*
> *che dice: "Fuggi, se'l perir t'è noia."*
> *Lo viso mostra lo color del core,*
> *che, tramortendo, ovunque pò s'appoia;*
> *e per la ebrietà del gran tremore*
> *le pietre par che gridin: Moia, moia.*
> 　*Peccato face chi allora mi vide,*
> *se l'alma sbigottita non conforta,*
> *sol dimostrando che di me li doglia,*
> *per la pietà che'l vostro gabbo ancide,*
> *la qual si cria ne la vista morta*
> *de li occhi, ch'hanno di lor morte voglia.*

What befalls me dies in my mind when I come to see you, beautiful joy; and when I am near you, I feel Love who says: "Flee, if to perish is irksome to you." My face shows the hue of my heart, which, fainting, leans for support wherever it may; and in the drunkenness of the great trembling the very stones seem to cry out: "Die, die." Then whoever beholds me sins if he does not comfort my frightened soul, showing that at least he feels sorry for me because of the pity which your mockery kills, and which is begotten in the dead light of my eyes which have desire of their own death.

And as for the *new* "matter" which the poet found after finishing these three sonnets, what is it if not precisely that other of the two established themes, that theme in praise of the lady of which we have seen outstanding examples already in the poems of Guinicelli and Cavalcanti? It seems indeed probable that, before the *Vita*

Nuova as a whole was conceived, Dante would already have written a number of sonnets on just this matter, sonnets such as that in chapter xxvi of the *Vita Nuova*:

> *Tanto gentile e tanto onesta pare*
> *la donna mia quand'ella altrui saluta,*
> *ch'ogne lingua deven tremando muta,*
> *e li occhi no l'ardiscon di guardare.*
> *Ella si va, sentendosi laudare,*
> *benignamente d'umiltà vestuta;*
> *e par che sia una cosa venuta*
> *da cielo in terra a miracol mostrare.*
>   *Mostrasi sì piacente a chi la mira,*
> *che dà per li occhi una dolcezza al core,*
> *che'ntender no la può chi no la prova:*
> *e par che de la sua labbia si mova*
> *un spirito soave pien d'amore,*
> *che va dicendo a l'anima: Sospira.*

So gentle and so modest my lady seems when she greets another that every tongue trembles and grows mute and eyes do not dare to look at her. She goes along, hearing herself praised, benignly clothed in humility; and she seems a thing come from heaven to earth to show a miracle. She is a sight so pleasant to anyone who sees her that through the eyes she sends a sweetness to the heart which cannot be understood by one who does not experience it; and from her face there seems to move a gentle spirit full of love that keeps saying to the soul: "Sigh."

Better than any other of the second group, that sonnet represents the second "matter" found by the poet, a matter which is also a manner.

But when poems are no longer single scattered things but have a place in a Book of Memory, then the very order of their occurrence in such a book can given them a new significance, especially if grouping is also a part of that order. For in that case (as a gloss in prose can make clear) the mere fact that one group follows another may also have special meaning. Poems become groups of poems for having a common subject matter. As subject matters emerge, a second can be new merely by leaving another behind. And change in matter is change in manner: the full implications of which fact

we shall not understand without examining the kinds of love from
which manners may arise.

*

*   *

The balance in outward arrangement noted between the first
and third *canzone* is maintained at the deeper level of subject matters. For just as the first *canzone* is the beginning of the second
subject matter and the end of the first, so now is the third *canzone*
the end of the second matter and the beginning of the third.

But what is this third matter? Actually, the sign of entrance
into it are the words from Jeremiah announcing the widowhood
of the city, as the prose of chapter xxx (is this number, made up
of three tens, another sign at this critical point?), which reconsiders
those words and gives their reason, tells us:

*Poi che fue partita da questo secolo, rimase tutta la sopradetta cittade
quasi vedova dispogliata da ogni dignitade; onde io, ancora lagrimando
in questa desolata cittade, scrissi a li principi de la terra alquanto de
la sua condizione, pigliando quello cominciamento di Geremia profeta
che dice:* Quomodo sedet sola civitas. *E questo dico, acciò che altri
non si maravigli perchè io l'abbia allegato di sopra, quasi come entrata
de la nuova materia che appresso vene.*

When she had departed from this world, all the aforesaid city remained as a widow bereft of all dignity; wherefore, still weeping in this
desolate city, I wrote to the princes of the earth somewhat of its condition, taking that beginning of Jeremiah the prophet which says: *Quomodo sedet sola civitas* [How doth the city sit solitary]. And I say this
so that no one will wonder that I have cited it above as an entrance to
the new subject matter which follows.

Our name for this third matter ought not to be simply "The
Death of Beatrice," but rather, "After the Death of Beatrice." For
the poems in it do not continue to look exclusively at the *object* of
love, and any fitting label for the new matter ought to allow for a
certain return to the focusing of the poems on the poet himself.
This third matter does begin with the cruel proclamation of Beatrice's death; but as it is developed by the poems of the third group
we realize that, like the first matter, this third is again concerned

with the lover and with the effects of love on him. Once more the
poems tend to be *narratori* of the state of the poet. Not that the
theme of praise is really abandoned, but it is no longer the exclusive
focus. The third matter is a blending of the other two themes into
a new one which includes them both and which, by doing so, transcends them. It is as a synthesis following on a thesis and an
antithesis. It becomes the two themes in one, showing the poet
at first thrown back upon himself and able to see only himself now
that Beatrice is gone; and, then, ending in forgetfulness of self, in
the triumph of a love which has found the way to a transcendental
place of rest, ending in a poet's resolve to praise his lady as no
lady was ever praised by poet.

Thus, for the three subject matters for poems in the *Vita
Nuova,* one might propose the following names:

    I. The effects of love on the poet.
    II. In praise of his lady.
    III. After the death of his lady.

But these, in any case, are only names for the subject matters of
poems, not for stages in love. As their causes, however, the stages
come first. For it is not, after all, the writing of poems which
makes a New Life, but the actual and very real upward progression
of the way of love in the poet who is the lover. However, that our
attention should first have fallen upon poems and subject matters
of poems is just as the Book of Memory would have it. The poems
are the first text. Then, from the gloss to the poems, we learn
that before the three subjects for poems were found, there were
three changes in the way of love which made for three stages in
love. Can the stages be named?

There are some fairly evident markers to guide us in the quest
of the answer. It is not hard, for instance, to say where the first
stage in love begins to end. That stage as such does not have, as
does the first subject, any precise signpost like a *canzone* to mark
its end; but that end can only be somewhere near the end of the
corresponding subject matter for poems; and in this regard the
denial of Beatrice's greeting appears to be the capital event. The

fact is evident enough from what the poet says to the ladies who are so curious over the end of his love:

Madonne, lo fine del mio amore fue già lo saluto di questa donna, forse di cui voi intendete, e in quello dimorava la beatitudine, chè era fine di tutti li miei desiderii. Ma poi che le piacque di negarlo a me, lo mio segnore Amore, la sua merzede, ha posto tutta la mia beatitudine in quello che non mi puote venire meno.

My ladies, the end of my love was once the greeting of this lady, whom perchance you have in mind, and in that dwelt beatitude, for it was the end of all my desires. But when it pleased her to deny it to me, my lord Love, through his grace, put all my beatitude in that which cannot fail me.

It is clear from these words how much a part of the change from one stage of love to another the denial of Beatrice's greeting is.

The poet, we recall, had brought this cruel moment upon himself. He had been far too assiduous in his efforts to make of the second "screen-lady" a cover for his love of Beatrice, and his attentions had resulted in much gossip on the part of malevolent people throughout the city. Whereupon, Beatrice, who was ever the queen of all virtues and the enemy of all evil things (of which this kind of gossip is one), one day refused the beatitude of her greeting to him who had brought about this unseemly talk.

Then we read in chapter xii that on the advice of the God of Love the poet wrote a *ballata* to his lady explaining how all this had come about, how it was all a mistake, how he had really been hers all the while. Nor are we given any reason to believe that Beatrice did not receive this poem. But if she did receive it, was there no jot of mercy in her? Why did she not forgive her lover? Why do we not read in the following chapter that Beatrice restored the greeting which it cost her so little to give and in which dwelt her lover's beatitude?

Merely to raise the question is to feel at once how irrelevant it is. There is only one reason why Beatrice's greeting was not restored, and this reason is not envisaged by such questions as those. It is simply that the denial of her greeting is a step in the upward way of love. It is because the lover must learn to do without that greeting that, in spite of all his explanations, it is never restored to him.

He is being taught that the beatitude and end of love is not really to be sought in such things as this, that true *salute* does not reside there. If love is to ascend, these things must be left behind for other things.

This is precisely a lesson which the poet seems to have learned by the time the ladies ask him about the end of his love. At just what moment between the refusal of her greeting and this meeting with those inquisitive ladies he had understood that, in spite of all apologies, the greeting was not to be restored to him, we do not know. But when we hear his reply to those ladies, it is evident that he already knows that this will be so. And, in knowing this, he has already stepped from the first stage of love to the second.

Moreover, we can see, from that same reply to the ladies, that this step from one to the other stage means primarily a change in his love (and of course an awareness of change) with respect to the *place* of the end of love. At first, the place of that end had been in the greeting of Beatrice. The greeting in itself we may take to be more than just an end for his love. It is a good symbol of any love which is turned toward satisfactions from without, any love which is interested in some return from the beloved, interested in reward. Such a love as this looking for some return from the beloved is one which the ladies who question the poet would not find at all unusual; nor, indeed, would it be unusual in the whole tradition of courtly love of which these questioning ladies are, in this instance, the mouthpiece. In troubadour love, the lover might always *hope* for reward from his lady, for some sign of "mercy" on her part, were this no more than a passing smile or a greeting. In fact, in that degree of refinement to which the conception of courtly love had by this time attained in Italy, some such sign of *mercè* was quite all in the way of reward that the lover might dare to expect.

The question which the ladies address to the poet assumes in fact that love will seek some reward from the beloved. That is why they are puzzled about the poet's love now, because they have all been present on occasions when it was evident that he was unable to endure even the presence of Beatrice. What can the end of love be, if the lover is never in a condition to receive a reward from the beloved?

A che fine ami tu questa tua donna, poi che tu non puoi sostenere la sua presenza? Dilloci, che certo lo fine di cotale amore conviene che sia novissimo.

To what end do you love this your lady, since you cannot endure her presence? Tell us this, for certainly the end of such a love must be most strange.

The ladies are thus bound to be all the more puzzled by the poet's answer to their question, which declares that the end and happiness of love is no longer in any reward which might come from Beatrice. Now, he says, thanks to the God of Love, the end and happiness of his love is put where it cannot fail him. Neither the ladies nor the tradition of troubadour love had ever heard of any such love as this. Where can the end of such a love as this be? "In those words which praise my lady," the poet replies.

It is the *place* of the end of love that counts. For the poet, now, the place of the end of his love could not have suffered a more radical transfer than this. And change there, moreover, must necessarily mean a change in the direction from which love's happiness comes, because the end of love is happiness. We must look at the matter in terms of *direction,* then, and it should now be clear that as long as all happiness came from the greeting of Beatrice, the direction of happiness was from the outside in. But now, if the happiness which is the end of love is in words which praise the beloved, the direction of the happiness of love must be the direction of just those words which arise in the poet and flow out toward the beloved. This is a complete reversal. Happiness now comes from within and flows from the inside out. What kind of love is this?

If we will turn for a moment to listen to Richard of St. Victor (d. 1173), a mystic whose work was well known to Dante, on the degrees of that love which is properly called *caritas,* we shall discover, I think, the right name for this second degree of love which the poet has reached in the *Vita Nuova.* Richard writes of what charity is (and is not) in terms of the direction of love:

Quomodo enim de amore loquetur homo qui non amat, qui vim non sentit amoris? De aliis nempe copiosa in libris occurrit materia; hujus vero aut tota intus est aut nusquam est, quia non ab exterioribus ad interiora suavitatis suae secreta transponit, sed ab interioribus ad exteriora transmittit. Solus proinde de ea digne loquitur qui secundum quod cor dictat verba componit.

For how shall one who does not love, who does not feel the power of love, speak of love? Now of other subjects abundant matter appears in books; but of this one, it is either entirely within or it is nowhere, because it does not transpose its hidden sweetness from the outside to the inside, but transmits it from the inside out. He alone, therefore, speaks of that subject worthily who, as his heart dictates, so composes his words.

Here let us remember that already in the line of progression from love to charity followed with regard to the object of love we had come to a point in the ascent where love was seen to become charity: where a God of Love was removed from the action, where all the authority of love was transferred to Beatrice, and Love itself was redefined.

Now, in the changes in a New Life in love as seen in the subject of love, we have come to a point at which we again see love becoming charity: where the new direction of love, in fact, is no longer to be distinguished from that of charity, if we may allow Richard's distinctions in terms of the direction of love to define that new direction for us. This we may surely do, for the happiness of love which may not fail the poet is a happiness arising within him and flowing outward, even as charity.

As is well known, love which is charity is a disinterested love having its final perfection in Heaven. Charity seeks no reward but, at the same time, charity is never without reward. The love of the blessed in Heaven finds its happiness in the contemplation of God and in praise of Him. In Heaven happiness arises within the soul and flows out to the Beloved. Evidently love of Beatrice in the new direction has reached a stage analogous to that.

Once more let us remember that, in that other line of progression from love to charity which was followed with respect to the object of love, charity was reached when the God of Love (who was the symbol of troubadour love) was removed from the action. Now in that parallel progression of the New Life as seen in the subject of love, we may observe in turn that when the greeting of Beatrice (which is likewise a sign of troubadour love) is removed from the action, a kind of love which may be called charity is reached. For a greeting as the end of love is the unmistakable symbol of a love which had never attained to disinterestedness, of a love ever hopeful of some *mercè* from the beloved. And that, precisely, is a predominant feature of troubadour love. However refined that love became, it continued to look for reward, some reward, from without. Now when the happiness of the poet's love has become a happiness arising freely within himself and flowing out from within, his love has ascended to a level above troubadour love—above because it is toward the perfection of love as love will be in Heaven—even though it is here still a love in this life.

A new direction in love means a new subject matter for poems of love. And this, if style be faithful to inspiration, means a new style in poetry.

Later on, in *Purgatory* xxiv, Dante will tell us as much and will give to this matter a dramatic cast, causing a poet of the older generation met there, a certain Bonagiunta from Lucca, to recognize in that first poem written to give expression to this new direction in love in the *Vita Nuova* (and to recognize in a redefinition of that direction) a style which is both new and sweet: *dolce stil nuovo*.

"Tell me," says Bonagiunta to Dante, who is standing before him on the terrace of the gluttons, "do I here behold him who produced the new rhymes beginning "Donne ch'avete intelletto d'amore?" This, as we know, is the first verse of the first *canzone* in the *Vita Nuova,* that first expression in verse of the second stage in the New Life in love as the Book of Memory has recorded it.

Dante replies to Bonagiunta's question with a definition in striking agreement with the one we heard Richard of St. Victor give of charity:

> *E io a lui: "I' mi son un che quando*
> *Amor mi spira, noto, e a quel modo*
> *ch'e' ditta dentro vo significando."*

And I to him: "I am one who, when Love inspires me, take note and, in the manner in which he dictates within, I proceed to signify."

To which the older poet replies:

> *"O frate, issa vegg'io," diss'elli, "il nodo*

che'l Notaro e Guittone e me ritenne
di qua dal dolce stil novo ch'i'odo!

Io veggio ben come le vostre penne
di retro al dittator sen vanno strette,
che de le nostre certo non avvenne."

"O friend, now I see," he said, "the knot which kept the Notary and Guittone and me short of that sweet new style which I hear. I see well how your wings follow closely after the dictator, which certainly did not happen to ours."

Now (now that he is in Purgatory where all souls are being schooled in the true nature of love which is charity), Bonagiunta understands what that knot was that kept him and the others he has named from attaining to that style (and understanding) of poetry which the first of the longer poems of the *Vita Nuova* represents. One even suspects that Bonagiunta is aware of the place of that poem in the Book of Memory. For only there is it the first of the poems on a new matter, only in its special place there does it represent a new style, because only there is it the expression of a changed direction in love. What the changed direction was we have seen, and we have found a definition and a name for it in Richard of St. Victor. The redefinition of it here in *Purgatory* only confirms our understanding. All of which means, if it means anything, that the first poem of the second group of poems in the *Vita Nuova* is the expression of a love which has found the direction of charity. And all this Bonagiunta seems now to understand, too.

We, in turn, may be expected to realize that the author of the poems of the *Vita Nuova* was himself at one time also "on the other side of the knot," had also kept company at one time with the poets of another generation. In fact, as long as he had written of a love which depended for its happiness on some return from without (on a beloved's greeting), he had written in the "old" style.

Thus we see that the order of the poems themselves in the Book of Memory, being the direct consequence of the order of the poet's love, makes a judgment on the relative merits of two styles. For since, as the Book of Memory has it, the order of love is an ascending one, any *new* matter for poems, merely by succeeding another, is of necessity more lofty than the preceding. If the ascent is toward perfection of love, then a second step must be nearer to the goal than the first. It must be more noble. And this the gloss in prose in the Book affirms it to be, telling us in chapter xvii that love at the second stage is a more noble matter for poems than at the first:

Poi che dissi questi tre sonetti, ne li quali parlai a questa donna, però che fuoro narratori di tutto quasi lo mio stato, credendomi tacere e non dire più, però che mi parea di me assai avere manifestato, avvegna che sempre poi tacesse di dire a lei, a me convenne ripigliare matera nuova e più nobile che la passata.

When I had composed these three sonnets in which I had spoken of this lady, since they were the narrators of nearly all my condition, thinking to be silent and write no more because it seemed to me that I had manifested enough of myself even though I should henceforth refrain from writing to her, it behooved me to take up a new and more noble subject matter than the last had been.

*

*   *

But it did not prove to be true that the poet's happiness had been put where it might not fail him. A second stage of love was not to be the last. He could not know that his love had not yet reached the place of its rest, which is the place of its greatest perfection, that his happiness had not yet attained to that place beyond change where it might endure.

The poet, in the first stage of the new life in love, had found all the happiness of his love to be in the greeting from his lady. Then, through the painful privation of that greeting, he had found the happiness to be within himself, welling up there and overflowing in praise of his lady. He had thought that such happiness as this might never be taken from him. How might it be, if he now bore its source within himself, if his love now resembled the love of the blessed in Heaven, being all contemplation of the Beloved and all praise of her? Is not self-sufficiency an inalienable attribute of such love as this?

But he could not then know that he had another even more painful lesson to learn. In the exultation of a new love which was already incipient charity, the poet had forgotten what must not be forgotten when the object of love is a mortal creature. For what if contemplation should be deprived of its object? Can the praise continue? Then will the happiness of love continue to arise within? What if Beatrice should die?

Apparently the motive force of a love which ascends, and which is transformed by changes in the place of its end, is privation itself. First it was the greeting which was taken from the poet, and this loss had brought him to the second stage of love. Then the loss became infinitely more: the loss was Beatrice herself. True, love in the second stage had no longer looked to the outside for any reward. But in contemplation of the Beloved it had, nevertheless, continued to look to the outside, to depend on an object of sensual contemplation, on the miraculous beauty of a living woman. However, when the poet had thought that such a happiness could not fail him, he had forgotten one thing: that death exists in the world. Then one day certain terrible words from Jeremiah took their place in the Book of Memory, and the poet knew that Beatrice was dead. Can even a disinterested love survive such privation as this?

*

*   *

The third matter for poems in the *Vita Nuova* is not, like the first and second, a theme already established in the tradition. Neither Guinicelli nor Cavalcanti had written poems on the death of the beloved. Of death in love they had written, but that was rather of the death which constantly menaced the lover in the overwhelming brightness of his lady's presence.

But the last subject matter of the poems in the *Vita Nuova* is the death of the Beloved. One should therefore note that, in the order given by a Book of Memory, not only is an evaluation made of two traditional themes for poetry, but these themes are surmounted there by a third which is not traditional and which gives a new significance to the other two as steps toward it.

Our modern mind is little given to considering events in terms of a final cause; of a cause, that is, which lies at the end of an event.

We are much more inclined to think of a cause as preceding what is caused, as being at the beginning rather than at the end. But the structure of a work of art (perhaps of any work of art) may still bring us to think in terms of that end cause to which medieval thought so readily turned. In the *Vita Nuova,* for instance, we must see the death of Beatrice, the last of three subject matters, as the cause of the other two. Actually, one feels little difficulty in allowing this in a sense, since it amounts only to saying something like this: if the last step in a flight of three steps reaches that point in space for which a stairway is intended, that point and hence that last step may be said to be the cause of the other two. This is, strictly speaking, not only a matter of order, but of their nature. The first would not only not be first, it would not even be the same step, if it were the only one; and even a first and a second step are different steps for having a step beyond them.

In the third stage, where is the place of the end of love? If the third subject matter is to be called "After the death of Beatrice," what shall the name of the third stage be, if that name, as in the case of the other two, is to be determined with regard to the place of the end of love?

In the third, the end is above. The final, the most noble resting place, and the last stage of the poet's new life in love is in Heaven. When we know the whole course of that new life (in so far as it is recorded in the Book of Memory) and can look back down over the ascending way, we feel certain that the only way in which that final place could have been attained was through the death of Beatrice.

*

*   *

But, for all that, love of Beatrice does not cease to be love of woman; and at this point, one may still with some profit persist in keeping an eye on the tradition in which the *Vita Nuova* is situated and ask: was any such circle as this completed anywhere else in the troubadour tradition?

In answering the question one ought to recall that when Guinicelli and Cavalcanti and other Italian poets of their time had written poems on the theme of praise, they had more than a few times regarded their ladies as miracles from Heaven. That is, with a hyperbole not surprising in such a deliberate theme of praise, the lady had many times been extolled as a creature sent from Heaven to earth to reveal here some of the splendor of God's kingdom. The figure of this *donna angelicata* implied thus a supernatural origin for love, a downward way of love from Heaven, the scheme of which is simple enough:

God
↓
donna
↓
poet

Only with the relatively late appearance in the tradition of the lady-as-angel did any such downward line emerge in clear outline. On the other hand, a line in the other direction, the outline of an upward way of love, was as old as the tradition itself. Courtly love, as we have seen, is never a love of equals. Madonna is always higher because she is *domina,* and the lover has always looked up to her simply because she was ever above him. The scale is not only amorous, it is moral. Being above, the lady had inspired the poet with virtue and the noblest of sentiments. Indeed it was she who made him the poet he was. Or, in the later development of this upward line, madonna was raised so high in the scale that as an object of love she was too much for mortal lover. The poet looks upward, but now the lady is so supernaturally bright that her lover falls, overcome by his love's too lofty and heavenly object. In this latter development it is evident that the one theme of praise which so lifted her would appear to have resulted in the theme of the effects of love. As the lady became more and more like an angel from Heaven, the effects of love for her on her lover had proved more and more disastrous. And this, as we have said, was the stage of development of the tradition when the *Vita Nuova* was written.

In terms of the two themes, then, the scheme may be extended so:

Theme of praise	Theme of effects
God	—
↓	
donna	donna
↓	↑
poet	poet

In the descending order (according to the theme of praise), love had come all the way from Heaven in the person of the lady. But in the ascent, love still came to rest at *madonna,* and in this remained faithful to the troubadour conception of love of woman. In fact, it was because love had stopped with madonna that finally, before God, there had had to be recantation of troubadour love. But that was before the *donna angelicata* so clearly emerged; that was when the object of love had not yet become as an angel from Heaven; and when our sketch of the downward way of love might not so surely be seen to begin with God.

But when the object of love had become as an angel and a miracle, and when a downward way of love from Heaven was so clearly suggested as it was in Guinicelli and his followers, should that not make a difference in the whole pattern? For if the lady is a gift of God, if she descends from Heaven, shall love of her not return to Heaven? In short, if the origin of love is supernatural, may not the end of love, by that very fact, be supernatural too?

It seems that Dante's first friend, Guido Cavalcanti, did not choose to see it so. In praising the lady as a miracle from Heaven, he had, of course, followed the lead of Guinicelli. Otherwise, Cavalcanti chose to keep the focus of the effects of love within natural bounds, as the troubadour tradition had always done. When he formulated a doctrine of love in that famous *canzone* already mentioned, Cavalcanti quite clearly insisted on seeing love as a natural phenomenon. In the vein of a theme of praise, his poems may have admitted, to be sure, that love seemed to come from Heaven. In this philosophical *canzone,* however, he does not appear to take that fact into serious account. In his poems, he was merely exploiting a situation inherited from Guinicelli, seeing (1) the beloved in the theme of praise as a miracle from Heaven, and (2) the effects of

love for such an object to be disastrous for the lover. Here then,
with Cavalcanti, is a love which is, as to its object, supernatural in
origin; and a love which, in the subject, does not rise above the
natural—and there precisely is a source of conflict in which he saw
the possibilities of a tragic love. He seems to have become the
champion of such a love which could know no rest and no satisfaction. For if love is movement seeking rest and joy, and if joy
is in union with the beloved, how can there ever be union (in the
natural order) with an object of love who is a miracle and whose
mere presence blinds the lover? Love, in such a situation, is necessarily a hopeless love, a love without possibility of peace.

Troubadour love was really always that—a love without peace.
Cavalcanti is merely heightening the paradox which that love had
always carried at its center. For if, by its own ideology, this love is
committed to remain always a love in which the object of love is
higher, how might there ever be any real union with such an object?
But now, to take her at the point of exaltation where Guinicelli had
left her, so much higher that her miraculous radiance blinded the
lover, is not the situation of love more hopeless than ever before?
But then, if love can never attain its end, must not either love or the
lover die? And, whether we take it from his lyrics or his philosophical poems, the words "Death often comes" are written large in
Cavalcanti's philosophy of love.

If, then, we imagine Guido Cavalcanti confronted by those ladies
of the *Vita Nuova* who one day stopped the poet to ask what the
end of love might be when the lover might not bear the presence
of the Beloved, we hear his clear answer: the end of such a love is
either death for love or death for the lover. For what the protagonist of the *Vita Nuova* had discovered to be the second stage in love,
Guido Cavalcanti did not grant: namely, that love, which is always
a movement, may be a disinterested movement from within, finding
its happiness and rest in pure contemplation and in praise. Cavalcanti's philosophy, in short, did not admit that the way of love might
extend beyond what is the initial stage of love in the scheme of the
Vita Nuova. He seems to have been unwilling in his philosophy
to allow that troubadour love of woman might endure and yet be
transcended.

Hence, against the more immediate background of its context in history, we see now more clearly than ever the tension which the *Vita Nuova* had in its time. And we understand, I think, by such a picture, why the *Vita Nuova* is written first of all for Guido Cavalcanti. The *Vita Nuova* takes a step which, in his doctrine of love, Cavalcanti would not take—a step by which the circle of a love which began in Heaven is completed. This is a new theory of love which should have interested a first friend!

And the important point is that the step which makes it a new theory is made possible by the death of Beatrice. The second stage of love in the *Vita Nuova* transcends certainly troubadour love and Cavalcanti's love; but that second stage does not suffice to point the way out. Death is the event which shows the real way out of the tragic position of Cavalcanti. But a poet may not simply affirm this to be so. He must see it concretely; and our copy from a Book of Memory is the seeing of it.

It ought to be remarked, however, that we draw our simple scheme of the "ascent" and "descent" of love, knowing all the while that Guinicelli's and Cavalcanti's talk of miracle from Heaven and of death for the lover is so much poetic rhetoric and a part of the convention of poetry. Even Thomas Aquinas agreed that it was natural for the lover to glorify his beloved. The "true" meaning of such praise of their ladies finds its control within the convention itself. But, if we attempt to look at the *Vita Nuova* in that way, we find it not quite the same thing. What we find in it we may not so easily discount as so much rhetoric. We are made in the *Vita Nuova* to feel that if any such discount of rhetoric had been necessary, the author himself would have performed it for us by declaring that this or that was not according to the truth, even as he did with a God of Love in his poems. That is, the poet of the *Vita Nuova* makes use of such figures as are allowed to poets, and in chapter xxv he defines their use. But there he also shows himself to be responsible *in prose* for the truth of what he says. Now if the miracle of Beatrice or his near death in her presence had also been figures of rhetoric like that of a God of Love, would the poet not have declared this too in the prose? It is precisely the prose of the *Vita Nuova* which brings in all its high seriousness.

One knows at the end of the *Vita Nuova,* that, as a theory of love, it was bent on reaching Heaven—nor is the word *Heaven* to be written in quotation marks. The whole work, from its first words, may be said to be aiming at Heaven—which is reached in its last words. At the end, it sees God—and this God is no figure which poets may use and writers of prose may not use. God is the living Christian God who may not be explained away as a rhetorical figure.

But, though we may see the prose itself as a surety of the complete earnestness of the whole, it is, actually, the third stage in love which clinches that beyond any question. And it is primarily the subject matter of the third stage which most does this. The effects of love on the lover and the praise of the lady belong to the tradition. The death of Beatrice does not. As the poet begins to make his copy out of the Book of Memory, Beatrice is already dead and in glory. This is no metaphor. It is the first fact on record in the prose, a record not written by human hand. It is, out of metaphor, not words, but reality. Indeed, a first reason why the complete seriousness of the *Vita Nuova* is beyond any question is that one of its authors—one of the authors of its prose—is God.

We are always led back to the fact that the little world of the *Vita Nuova* (without the prose it would not be a little world) is open at the top. There, at the top, God's light enters. And it is none other than that same light *which lighteth every man that cometh into the world.*

*

* *

Beatrice herself is a gift of God. Even as she came from Heaven, she returns to Heaven. But just how may love of her be said to lead to Heaven? The last sonnet of the *Vita Nuova* is the answer to the question:

> *Oltre la spera che più larga gira*
> *passa 'l sospiro ch'esce del mio core:*
> *intelligenza nova, che l'Amore*
> *piangendo mette in lui, pur sù lo tira.*

Quand'elli è giunto là dove disira,
vede una donna, che riceve onore,
e luce sì, che per lo suo splendore
lo peregrino spirito la mira.
　Vedela tal, che quando 'l mi ridice,
io no lo intendo, sì parla sottile
al cor dolente, che lo fa parlare.
So io che parla di quella gentile,
però che spesso ricorda Beatrice,
sì ch'io lo'ntendo ben, donne mie care.

Beyond that sphere which has the largest orbit, the sigh passes which issues from my heart: a new intelligence which Love, weeping, puts into it draws it ever upward. When it arrives where it desires, it sees a lady who is being honored and who so shines that by her splendor this pilgrim spirit looks at her. It sees her such that when it tells me I do not understand, so subtly does it speak to the sorrowing heart which makes it speak. I know that it speaks of that gentle lady because it often mentions Beatrice, so that I understand it well, my dear ladies.

Here now is a way of going to Heaven quite different from that of the *Divine Comedy.* In *Paradiso,* the poet really goes to where God is (though whether in the body or not he does not know). In the *Vita Nuova,* only a sigh makes the journey, a sigh which leaves the poet's heart and finds its upward way to Heaven. This difference is a good measure of the distance which separates these two itineraries to God. Both the *Comedy* and the *Vita Nuova* are actions having their beginnings and their ends in Heaven, both are actions having Beatrice as guide. But at the end of the *Paradiso,* Beatrice is no longer between the poet and God: she has gone to take her seat among the Blessed, and at the end of the *Comedy* the poet faces God directly. But, in the *Vita Nuova,* only a sigh makes the journey to Heaven; and that sigh meets with Beatrice there, it seems, not with God. This does not mean that Beatrice is the terminus of the way of love. God is that. Beatrice is the way to God in the *Vita Nuova* even as in *Paradiso.* Only, in the *Vita Nuova,* she does not step aside. She remains there in the medial position between her lover and God to the very end. Charity, says a contemporary of St. Bernard, is the eye that sees God. And it is the last sigh of the poet of the *Vita Nuova* that he may one day see his lady who now sees God.

Thus, the range of difference at the end of the two works is very great and should not be underestimated. It means all the difference between being finally in Heaven where we shall see God directly and being finally still on this earth where we may know Him only through His creatures and by analogy.

Nor must we think of the New Life in love as ending with the closing words of the *Vita Nuova*. We are not told that more will not be written down under the rubric headed *Incipit Vita Nova*. We know from this copy only the beginning of the New Life.

*

*　　*

In both the *Paradiso* and the *Vita Nuova,* Beatrice is the guide along a way which reaches to where God is. With all due allowance for differences, it may still be said that the force which bears the poet upward is, in either case, the same. That force is a love which first moved from Heaven and which lifts from there; and those same verses in *Paradiso* (I, 124-126) in which Beatrice explains to her charge what that force is, we may appropriately take to apply to the *Vita Nuova* as well:

> *E ora lì come a sito decreto*
> *cen porta la virtù di quella corda*
> *che ciò che scocca drizza in segno lieto.*

And now there as to a place decreed we are borne away by the power of that cord which directs whatever it shoots to a. happy target.

There, of course, means Heaven. There is where the Archer is. From there He shoots the arrow which is aimed at Him. He is the final cause of love. In Him alone is the circle of love completed.

In this same passage in *Paradiso*, Beatrice continues the figure of the archer and the bow with an argument which we shall do well to bring to bear on the interpretation of a dramatic episode in the *Vita Nuova:* the poet's momentary infatuation with a certain lady who had shown pity for him in his grief over the loss of Beatrice.

> Vero è che come forma non s'accorda
> molte fiate all'intenzion dell'arte,
> perch'a risponder la materia è sorda;
>
> così da questo corso si diparte
> talor la creatura c'ha podere
> di piegar, così pinta, in altra parte.
>
> E sì come veder si può cadere
> foco di nube, sì l'impeto primo
> l'atterra torto da falso piacere.

True it is that just as form does not agree many times with the intention of the art because matter will not respond, just so from this course sometimes the creature deviates who has the power, so impelled, to bend another way. And just as fire can be seen to fall from a cloud, so does the first impulse turn itself toward earth, deflected by false pleasure.

Here is an account which may be seen to explain very well what happened in the *Vita Nuova* when the poet forgot Beatrice and allowed his love to turn toward a "compassionate lady." Not only in *Paradiso* but in the *Vita Nuova,* too, Beatrice is the means by which a love which begins in Heaven lifts the poet toward the point of that love's origin and its final cause. In either work, Beatrice is the arrow, a missile of divine love which, being shot from Heaven, will return to Heaven. But her lover is a creature endowed with a will capable of changing its course (since it is free), and when death takes Beatrice away, her lover is thrown back upon himself and his own free will: a will which up to now had been bound in love of her but is now free; but precisely because it is free, it is unable to make the right choice. Without guidance from above, it bends away from the upward path, deflected by false pleasure.

The poet's Reason loudly protests this deflection, and between Reason and Appetite a struggle ensues. The words deserve their capital initials for, in this brief struggle over the direction of the poet's love, the faculties which they name are almost personified. Reason, we see, can resist Appetite perfectly well; but Reason, alone and unaided, may not set the poet's love back on its right way. Only a help which comes from Heaven may do this, and that help comes in the *Vita Nuova* even as it does to the dark wood of *Inferno*. For, in the *Vita Nuova,* a strong "imagination" one day comes to the poet, bringing into his mind again the image of Beatrice. Once more he sees her as she was on that day when she first appeared before him dressed in red. Reason at least has managed to hold the fortress until this help could arrive. Now that it has come, the upward way of love is assured of reaching its final goal. Guidance from Heaven is restored, the arrow has again found its path, and there can now be no doubt that the circle of love will be successfully completed in Heaven.

This second time the image of Beatrice had come as grace. But Beatrice, even so, does not cease to be charity. Even here, where she is so clearly grace, the color of her gown keeps the other meaning. For the color of charity is red. But the other name for a created charity which comes once again from Heaven to lift up one who is lost is grace.

*

*   *

Three stages in love, three subject matters for poems: the new life, as the Book of Memory has recorded it, is itself a "song of degrees." The expression is St. Augustine's. It can remind us, though, that the ordering of love in the new life shows a considerable resemblance to the ordering of love as the Saint had expressed it in his *Confessions:*

We ascend Thy ways that be in our heart and we sing a song of degrees; we glow inwardly with Thy good fire and we go because we go upward to the peace of Jerusalem.

A mystic tradition of the Middle Ages, well nourished on Augustine, had spoken of the ascent of the mind and heart to God as an ascent by degrees. There was also general agreement that these degrees were three. Sometimes they were named the *purgative,* the *illuminative,* and the *unitive,* but the names might change. What is fairly constant is the number three. This itinerary of the mind to God, as Augustine had conceived it, began, at its first level, *outside* of man. It turned *inward* at its second level or degree. And

in its third and last stage, it rose *above* man. St. Bonaventura, in
Dante's own century, is still tracing much the same pattern. In
his *Itinerarium mentis in Deum* the stages, as with Augustine, bear
the names of *extra nos, intra nos,* and *supra nos.*

We have seen what the position of the lover is, even at the end
of the New Life. It is the position of a man still in this life, whose
love stretches out to Heaven from earth. That is precisely the situation of the mystic's love of God. It was an "excess of the mind," a
"stretching out of love." When Augustine and Bonaventura speak
of the journey to God, they mean it as a possibility in this life.
It is for this reason especially that the pattern of the ascent of love
in the *Vita Nuova* can so closely resemble the pattern of the mystic
ascent to God.

Many readers of the *Vita Nuova* have recognized that this resemblance is most apparent in the third stage of the new life in love
of Beatrice. In the final sonnet of the book, it is especially clear.
The contemplative lover of God knew that he could not attain to
that holy and mysterious moment of union for which all his love
yearned unless help came from above and lifted him to the happiness of a peace so far above him and his mortal condition. A power
from on high (call it Love or Charity or Grace, for it is all of these)
must infuse his mind with a new intelligence if the last step is to
be possible at all.

These three steps in the order of love were thus closely parallel
to those in the order of knowledge of things divine, as St. Thomas
outlines them:

Man has three kinds of knowledge of divine things. The first of
these is according as man, by the natural light of reason, ascends through
creatures into the knowledge of God; the second is in so far as the divine
truth, exceeding human understanding, descends to us by way of revelation, not however as though demonstrated to our sight, but as set forth
in words to be believed; and the third is according as the human mind
is elevated to the perfect intuition of the things that are revealed.

But the true mystic, though at times he may seem to be speaking
of such a way in knowledge, really means to describe a way in love.
And the way as set forth in the last sonnet of the *Vita Nuova* is
beyond any doubt the way of love and not the way of knowledge.

Indeed, it is so much so that the ascent to Heaven is only that of a sigh mounting upward from the poet's heart, lifted by a new "intelligence" which love puts into it.

If the resemblance to the way of mystic love is thus so striking at the end, one is encouraged to turn back over the whole way of love in the new life and ask if that likeness is not to be seen there throughout the whole. The first two stages of love in the new life might also correspond to the first two in the mystic pattern.

The greeting of Beatrice, and her lover's dependence on it for all his happiness, is the sign and expression of the first stage of love in the *Vita Nuova.* Love is a movement in the soul. A new life in love is new because, in it, love is ordered and reordered (renewed) toward an end, the direction of love being determined, as we have said, by the place of the end. Now, when the end of love is the greeting of Beatrice, which is what defines the first stage of love in the New Life, does not that stage, by that very fact, agree with the first of the mystic way in which love turns first of all to the *outside;* in which, as Augustine and Bonaventura say, the end is *extra nos?* And when the poet, deprived of the greeting, finds that the end of love can no longer be *extra,* when he discovers that the happiness which is the end of love arises *within* himself, has he not passed to a stage of love which may very well bear the name which the mystic gave to his own second stage: *intra nos?* And, finally, may there be any mistake about the name for the third stage of love in the *Vita Nuova?* Is that not clearly *supra nos?*

The three stages of love in the New Life, even though they are not explicitly named, bear such an unmistakable resemblance to the mystic stages that they might also bear their names.

As for names, St. Bonaventura's *Itinerary* supplies us with yet another for the first of the three stages:

Secundum hunc triplicem progressum mens nostra tres habet aspectus principales. Unus est ad corporalia exteriora, secundum quem vocatur animalitas *seu sensualitas.*

According to this triple progression our mind has three main directions [aspects]. One is toward external material things, and is accordingly called *animalitas* or *sensualitas.*

Animalitas. If, out of analogy with the mystic pattern, the first
stage in the New Life may bear any such name as this, then we see
in that fact yet another reason why a second stage of love may be
more noble than the first. And since love in that first stage of the
New Life recognizes its total dependence on a greeting from
Beatrice (which is obviously an end both corporeal and external), it
would seem that that first stage might deserve just such a name.

But then, if this be admitted, we shall also be obliged to recall
that the first stage of love in the *Vita Nuova* was identical with the
conception of love of woman according to the troubadour tradition,
and how, in more than one way, one saw that when the poet had
learned that the happiness of love is not *extra* but *intra,* he had left
troubadour love behind him and attained to a love which is charity.
Hence, if that first stage may by such transfer bear the name of
animalitas, so too must all love of woman as the troubadours had
conceived it.

It is in keeping with the mystic experience of rapture and union
with God that the sigh which finally reaches Heaven may not long
remain where Beatrice is, and may not say, on its return, what its
experience there has been. The mind of one still in this life may
not long endure such rapture. This is that blessed half hour at
the end of the mystic journey when there is silence in Heaven.
But the weight of mortality easily breaks in upon that silence and
the rapture soon falls away. When it is gone, words may not
express what it has been. So the last sonnet of the *Vita Nuova* tells
us, so again the first canto of *Paradiso:*

> *Nel ciel che più de la sua luce prende*
> *fu'io e vidi cose che ridire*
> *nè sa nè può chi di là sù discende.*

In the heaven which receives His light the most was I, and saw
things which one who returns from there has neither the knowledge or
the power to retell.

And further along in the same canto:

> *Trasumanar significar per verba*
> *non si poria.*

To go beyond the human may not be signified in words.

Trasumanar. This, in the *Vita Nuova* and in the *Divine Comedy,* is the final stage of a love that goes upward toward Heaven. And only if such transcendence of self is possible may either the lover of God or the lover of Beatrice know the peace of Jerusalem.

The third and last stage which St. Bonaventura distinguishes in the mystic itinerary he designates as follows:

Tertius [aspectus] supra se, secundum quem dicitur mens.

The third [direction] is above ourselves, which is accordingly called *mens.*

Mens. Here again, if we allow Bonaventura's name to be the name for the corresponding stage in the new life in love of Beatrice, we ought now to recall what we have seen to be the nature of the form of the *Vita Nuova,* how it ends where it begins, with Beatrice dead and now in the glory of eternal life, with Beatrice already *supra nos* at that place where love will come into the knowledge of its last perfection. The word *gloriosa* in the first sentence in the book tells us this. And what St. Bonaventura tells us about the place of the perfection of love and its name, the whole of that phrase in which the word *gloriosa* occurs, tells us too:

La gloriosa donna della mia mente.

V

Beatrice Dolce Memoria

THE very fact that the new life has its model in the mystic itinerary to God ought of itself to contribute to and control our general understanding of the nature of the *Vita Nuova*. It is precisely this relationship of a copy to such a model that alone argues strongly against the intention of allegory in the copy. For in the model, allegory is not found. When the mystic drew the outline of the ascent of the mind and heart to God, one may wonder that he did not use allegory, since he intended the pattern he drew to have a certain validity for man in general, certainly for the mind of more than one man. But the fact is that he did not choose the allegorical method. And when mystics, on the other hand, spoke not of any general scheme of ascent, but rather of their own personal experience of the supreme moment of transcendence and union with God, their account was then far removed from even the possibility of allegory. For it is of the essence of this experience to be unique and personal; not general, because not predictable, any more than is grace itself, since only by the descent of grace from God may the ascent of the mind to union with God occur at all.

One of the greatest of the mystics begins a sermon with the words *Hodie legimus in libro experientiae,* words which might properly be inscribed over each and every account of the actual experience of the upward journey of the mind to God. Even St. Augustine, though he did not do so, could well have written those words at the top of the first page of the *Confessions.* He, too, was reading in the book of experience, and those great contemplatives who followed in the pathways which he so passionately sought and found continued to consult the same book he had used.

The Book of Memory is obviously the counterpart of just that "book of experience." It, too, is the record of a unique experience in which grace counted for everything.

If Beatrice had not been a miracle and a gift of God, what is reported in the Book of Memory could never have been. And that Beatrice was such a miracle and such a gift we may not doubt—not, that is, if we have understanding of love (and we are told repeatedly that this copy is made only for those who do); which means that we have understanding of the tradition and know that, as a miracle, Beatrice is not unique. Guinicelli and Cavalcanti and the other poets had each claimed as much for his own lady. If we have understanding of love, we shall know that the *donna angelicata* who is a gift of God is a *datum* of the tradition, and that, therefore, Dante does not have to beg us to believe that Beatrice is a miracle. A poet has a right to begin with what the tradition provides.

Neither in the poems of the others nor in Dante's early poems is the *donna angelicata* an allegorical figure. Nor is Beatrice made to be such a figure in the *Vita Nuova.* Like the ladies of those other poets, Beatrice is a creature, a wondrously beautiful individual of flesh and blood who lived once in time. In the *Vita Nuova* we see her die. Beatrice will not happen again. Let us for the moment forget the allegories of the *Convivio,* and let us forget Beatrice as she is in the *Comedy.* For there Beatrice unquestionably becomes an allegory, though she does not, for that, cease to be the person she was in the *Vita Nuova.* But in the *Vita Nuova,* Beatrice has no *other* name which may be spelled with a capital initial. She is neither Grace nor Charity, though she wears the color of the latter and descends from Heaven like the former. She is a creature, a mortal woman bearing her mortality like the rest of us; and she is a miracle and a gift of God, as the tradition (and perhaps more than the tradition) allowed her to be: creature and miracle. One can take it or leave it. But one had better take it, for if one does not, the *Vita Nuova,* as a theory of love, will not come out right. There is this to be said about it, however: one has no particular difficulty in taking it, if one will but submit to the form of the *Vita Nuova,* since the whole book is constructed to reveal just that— that Beatrice is a miracle and a gift of God.

Beatrice (as the God of Love declares) is love, which, in view of what is revealed about her true nature, can mean only that she is a love which comes from God. She is a created love which must be charity, created charity, coming as she does from Heaven. But neither is this name to be spelled with a capital initial. For Beatrice is only a particular instance of created charity. Before she was, there were certainly other manifestations of God's love on earth, and there have been others since. This is surely no allegory. Nor would anyone feel inclined to argue the point at such length, now that we have seen what Beatrice must be in the *Vita Nuova,* if only we might forget that abundant record of our propensity to mistake the matter which is found in Dante literature.

But if Beatrice is no allegory, she is not without a kind of "other" meaning, as any attentive reader of the book is bound sooner or later to see. He will not, in fact, go beyond chapter xxiv without meeting face to face with this "other" meaning of Beatrice. It is what at first sight appears to be a resemblance of Beatrice to Christ, stressed so emphatically in that chapter and so impressively seen again at her visionary death. It is a resemblance which our present reading has called both an analogy and a metaphor, and which is, we have argued, as we looked upon the *Vita Nuova* as an artifact, the central and controlling principle of the whole construction. But now that we have glimpsed here and there the variety of ways in which this resemblance appears throughout the whole, we may perhaps look back upon it with fuller understanding.

Indeed, now we may see that this is actually no resemblance of the person of Beatrice to that of Christ. Neither in character nor appearance would the one suggest the other. Nor would we expect this to be so. Between the two is an infinite gulf, the distance between God and the creature. No principle of close resemblance of any creature to Christ will hold in view of that distance. This resemblance results rather from a likeness to be seen not between two persons but between two actions: that is, the action in which Beatrice has the role which her name itself implies (a bringer of beatitude) is like the action in which Christ has such a role. Both are actions leading to *salute,* to the beatitude of Heaven. And in the one Beatrice *is,* as Christ *is* in the other: a love which comes from Heaven and returns, *through death,* to Heaven. The actions are two, the roles in the actions are two, and no degree of equivalence is affirmed.

Nor may the one replace the other. But this they do have in common: each action admits at the top the same light of Heaven. The
same living Christian God is the final goal of both. This is clearly
what may properly be called analogy. But the fact that the two
lines of action have a common terminus is important for saying
what kind of analogy this is.

It may remind us, indeed, that if we should attempt to conceive
of these two actions as taking place on two different stages, we are
wrong. For here are two actions, each reaching upward through
death to beatitude. At the center of one is Christ on the Cross, dying in the ninth hour. At the center of the other is Beatrice, dying
in a vision which came on the ninth day of a fever. But these two
dramas must take place on the same stage, for the Heaven above
them both is the same Heaven, and the God above them both is the
same God, and the beatitude which is their end is not different in
kind, but only in degree.

What the stage is on which the Passion stands at the center there
may be no doubt. It is simply the stage of this whole world as the
Middle Ages conceived it, the stage upon which the only possible
drama that mattered was forever reënacting itself in time, that
drama of salvation in which no one of us might refuse to act his
part. The stage includes everything, heaven and earth and time
itself, which had a beginning and will have an end; and the play
upon it is the fulfillment of an eternal idea.

And that other play, with Beatrice dying at its center, is acted
out upon this same stage; but it is an action so infinitely smaller
that, were our eyes not focused on it by the pages of a certain Book
of Memory, we should not see it. It does not involve all men. It
organizes itself around a creature, in fact, not around the Son of
Man; and it concerns not the beatitude of all men, but only the
beatitude of one man, the lover of Beatrice. Neither does Beatrice
die in order to save him, as Christ dies for all men. No. When
Beatrice dies, only a creature dies—a creature who is a miracle.
But it is nonetheless true that without her removal through death
from the scene of this world, her lover's love would not have attained to the place of its perfection and rest. Between the two
actions there is no possibility of equivalence, but there is no denying

an analogy. It is what the Middle Ages would have recognized as an *analogy of proportion*.

But if this is analogy, it is only such a one as may enter into a work of art. For the term "analogy" must not suggest that the *Vita Nuova* is any abstract formulation. The *Vita Nuova* sees as poems see, not as mathematics sees, or logic.

For the *Vita Nuova* is a theory of love, to be sure—but theory in an original sense of the word: a *beholding* of how things may be, and, in this case, how they may be in the order of their *rightness*. Dante, like the other poets of his generation, had written poems on themes inherited from Guinicelli and the tradition. But until he chose to surround certain of those poems with a prose controlling their meaning and ordering it toward an end, Dante had not faced the problem of whether love of woman, as the poems of Guinicelli and Cavalcanti and his own poems had represented it, might or might not be seen as good love, might or might not be seen in reference to and in subordination to love of God. And that is the problem which the *Vita Nuova,* as theory, faces and sees through. By making its beginning in the cult of troubadour love, with a God of Love and faithful servants of love who are poets each with his wondrous madonna, the *Vita Nuova* acknowledges its responsibility, sets up its problem resolutely. And the work ends facing God as no other beginning in troubadour love had ever done or would ever do—without recantation. The unique achievement of the *Vita Nuova* as a theory of love is the seeing how love of woman may be kept all the way up to God.

*

*   *

To see such an action recorded in a Book of Memory is to see it as having taken place in time. It might have meant to see it as a fact of history. But we are not shown a Book of Memory directly. A gloss is added to what is copied from that Book, and by that gloss the pages are interpreted for us. Already in the original there was a gloss. This means two movements, as it were, through the book. One is simply the line of events in the order of their occurrence, a forward movement carried by the poems and by the narrative connecting them. The other is a reflective movement back over those events, a movement seeking to understand them, to discover that by which they become something more than fact, become intelligible. This the gloss as gloss serves to carry out.

Fact alone would have given an account of his life in love of Beatrice—these poems themselves arranged in a certain order would almost have given that. But it seems fairly certain that the events as fact were not what most interested the author of the *Vita Nuova.* For him, fact, to have significance, must reveal an intelligible order. For him, love of woman—even of a woman whose name was Beatrice—must reveal an order of rightness to be good love, which is a love needing no recantation before God. Was love of Beatrice good love? Could it be seen as such? The whole of the *Vita Nuova* is the answer.

And the eye which has so passionately sought that answer has looked steadily at the fact until it has seen in that circle, which love of Beatrice described between Heaven and earth, the reflection of another circle, the eternal circle of Christian love; has looked until in that little world of events, which constituted the beginning of a new life in love of Beatrice, could be seen the reflection of the eternal idea of Christ. Then and only then has that little world of love found the touchstone by which its reality as good love can be known. A reality of idea, not of fact. Then and only then does one understand the full meaning of the rubric in the Book of Memory: *Incipit Vita Nova;* for then one hears the echo of that other idea of a life made new by love:

> *Propter quod non deficimus; sed licet is qui foris est, noster homo corrumpatur, tamen is qui intus est renovatur de die in diem. . . Caritas enim Christi urget nos; aestimantes hoc, quoniam si unus pro omnibus mortuus est, ergo omnes mortui sunt; et pro omnibus mortuus est Christus, ut et qui vivunt, jam non sibi vivant, sed ei qui pro ipsis mortuus est et resurrexit. Itaque nos ex hoc neminem novimus secundum carnem. Et si cognovimus secundum carnem Christum, sed nunc jam non novimus. Si qua ergo in Christo nova creatura, vetera transierunt:* ecce facta sunt omnia nova. *(II* Ad Corinthios, *IV, 16; V, 14-17.)*

For which cause we faint not; but though our outward man perish, yet the inward man is renewed day by day. . . For the love of Christ constraineth us; because we thus judge, that if one died for all, then were all dead: And that he died for all, that they which live should not henceforth live unto themselves, but unto him which died for them and rose again.   Wherefore henceforth know we no man after the flesh; yea, though we have known Christ after the flesh, yet now henceforth know we him no more.   Therefore if any man be in Christ, he is a new creature: old things are passed away; behold, all things are become new.

*

*   *

For us, too, the measure of the validity of a work of art is our sense of the necessity of its form. And once we have grasped the first principle by which love of Beatrice is intelligible as good love, we have glimpsed that center of a work of art which is not ever literally the center, because it can be found in no one place but is everywhere felt. Then we have understood what even the Middle Ages, indeed, what especially the Middle Ages, would consider to be *form*—that hidden principle of life from which all the rest follows.

Even so, we may still wonder if we have seen or felt the whole necessity of the way in which that form has its existence. Why should the image of Christ shine through the pages of a Book of Memory? Why there? Is there perhaps a way by which we may see a necessary connection between that image of a Book of Memory which controls the outward form of the *Vita Nuova* and that analogy with Christ which is the principle of its inner form? In other words, can inner form be seen to give outward form?

It can. A hymn attributed to St. Bernard and well known to Dante's century can help us to see this. Its opening words are these: *Jesu dulcis memoria.*

And as we read that hymn we realize that the death of Jesus Christ could be conceived as a presence, a sweet presence, in the memory; that Christ on the Cross could be thought of as standing at the center of *all* books of memory. So that it was no arbitrary, no unnecessary, vision on the part of the author of the *Vita Nuova* when he saw the image of the Saviour shining through the pages of his own Book of Memory, whereon was recorded a song of degrees in praise of another bright image present in memory, even in death.

Notes

A GREAT deal has been written on the *Vita Nuova;* so much, indeed, that by now it is nearly impossible to hold any opinion on its interpretation without discovering in the mass of writing which has accumulated about it at least a dozen views in some measure opposed to one's own. But to go forth in these notes to meet these many opposing positions would amount to writing another volume much larger than the present one. And this I have readily decided against. For even though it may have originated in a spirit of polemic, this essay has in time outgrown its origin. To Theodore Spencer of Harvard University, who was kind enough to read it in manuscript, I owe thanks, I believe, for making me aware of that fact.

These notes, therefore, are that bare minimum which even the casual reader would have a right to expect. They do little more than document assertions, assign sources, and acknowledge all that I am aware of having used from the work of the many who have written on the *Vita Nuova* and on the Middle Ages.

It was not possible to acknowledge in these notes a quite special debt owed to Leo Spitzer, colleague at the Johns Hopkins University—a debt of the kind that is hard to distinguish and hard to declare because contracted through a daily association in scholarship and friendship for over ten years.

For the *Vita Nuova* I have used the critical text of Michele Barbi in his last edition of the work (Firenze, 1932: Edizione nazionale delle opere di Dante, vol. I). For the other works of Dante, my references, unless otherwise noted, are to the text as given by the editors of the Società dantesca: *Le opere di Dante* (Firenze, 1921), in one volume. *PL* indicates the *Patrologie latine* of Migne.

All translations from Italian and Latin works in the essay or in the following notes are my own, unless otherwise declared.

Since the present essay is intended first of all for readers who seek to understand and enjoy the *Vita Nuova* in and for itself, I have preferred not to distract them by numbered references to these

117

notes in the text of the essay. On the other hand, those readers who are interested in what must be relegated to the notes will have no difficulty, I think, in finding the points to which they refer, as this is made plain by a reference to the relative page of the text and by some words from the text as an additional guide.

Pages 3-4

The quotation is from Emile Mâle, *Religious Art in France, XIII Century,* translated from the third edition (revised and enlarged) by Dora Nussey (London: J. M. Dent, 1913), p. vii. The reference is to Molanus, *De historia sanctarum imaginum et picturarum,* the first edition of which appeared in 1580.

Page 4

For the 1576 edition of the *Vita Nuova,* and for a more detailed account of the changes which it introduced into the text, see M. Barbi's introduction to his critical edition of the *Vita Nuova,* pp. xc-xci. See also P. Toynbee, "The Inquisition and the Editio Princeps of the *Vita Nuova,*" *Modern Language Review* (1908), pp. 228-231.

Page 4

Salus. See Psalms (Vulg.) XXVI, 1: *Dominus illuminatio mea et salus mea;* LXXIII, 12: *Operatus est salutem in medio terrae;* and for the gloss, St. Bernard, *Sermones in cantica, PL* 183, 1014: *Unus est enim vitae auctor, unus mediator Dei et hominem, homo Christus Jesus qui dicit sponsae suae: Salus tua ego sum* (Psalms XXIV, 3). See also Alanus de Insulis, *Liber in distinctionibus,* etc., *PL* 210, 932: "*Salus,* propie. Dicitur sanitas corporis, unde David: *et fallax equus ad salutem,* id est temporalis potentia non potest homini conferre sanitatem vel conservare. Dicitur puritas mentis, unde David: *Domine Deus salutis meae* Dicitur vita aeterna, unde Psalmista: *Salus autem justorum a Domino;* ipse etiam Deus dicitur salus, quia est causa salutis, unde David: *Dominus illuminatio mea et salus mea, quem timebo?*" Note also here, immediately following: "*Salutare* propie Christus per quem salus; unde Jacob: *salutare tuum expectabo.*"

Page 5

Usage in Dante's time made it possible to express the meaning "greeting" or "salutation" with both *il saluto* and *la salute.* Only the former has survived in this sense, whereas *la salute* could still bear that meaning and that of "health" and (hence) "salvation." This was true also of *la salut* in Old Provençal. See A. Schiaffini, *Tradizione e poesia* (Genova, 1934), pp. 145-146.

Page 6

Beatrice, beatrice. I refer, of course, to the much-debated end of the first sentence of the *Vita Nuova* proper (chapter II): *la gloriosa donna de la mia mente, la quale fu chiamata da molti Beatrice li quali non sapeano che si chiamare.* The meaning of this I take to be: *the glorious lady of my mind, who was called Beatrice by many who did not know what her name was.* One might of course print *beatrice* here in the text (see L. Spitzer, *Bemerkungen zu Dantes "Vita Nuova"* [Publications de la faculté des lettres de l'Université d'Istanbul; Istanbul, 1937], pp. 162-169: "Zur Verwendung des Namens Beatrice"), since the common noun meaning "one who blesses" is here to the fore; and yet, the marvel is that in calling her *beatrice* they were also saying *Beatrice,* which was her true name. Editors will do well, therefore, to hold to the form *Beatrice* here in the text.

As for the construction *non sapeano che si chiamare,* I see no reason that it should present any more difficulty than, for instance, that of *non sapevano che si fare,* a construction not too rare in Italian.

Page 6

Beatrice a mortal creature. Cf. Guido Cavalcanti's sonnet to Guido Orlandi beginning *La bella donna, dove Amor si mostra,* vs. 9-12:

> Ch'ell'è per certo di sì gran valenza,
> che già non manca in lei cosa da bene
> ma' che natura la creò mortale.

Page 7

Inferno, XI, 105: *sì che vostr'arte a Dio quasi è nipote.*

Page 13

Visions not understood at the time. This, of course, is a common feature in the experience of visions and prophetic dreams, and many examples of it are easily adduced, apart from the obscurity of Christ's utterances regarding his death, which, as I shall say further on, I hold to be the real informing principle here. See Genesis (Vulg.) XXXVII, 6-8

and 9-11; also XLI, 11: *audivimus quidquid postea rei probavit eventus.*
As for a protagonist who is never actually shown to have understood later,
one ought to remember the prophetic dreams in *Purgatorio* (which are
also three). Neither is the protagonist there, at any point further
along in the poem, brought to reflect on their prophetic nature; and
yet, with the event of what comes, the reader knows that they were
prophetic and knows that the protagonist would also have known.
For the prophetic dream, see Thomas Aquinas, *Summa theologica,*
II-II, 95, 6, obj. 3 under the article *Utrum divinatio quae fit per somnia
sit illicita:*

> Praeterea, illud quod communiter hominis experiuntur, irrationabile est
> negare. Sed omnes experiuntur somnia habere aliquam significationem
> futurorum. Ergo vanum est negare somnia habere vim divinationis. Ergo
> licitum est eis intendere.

Page 14

A poem by Guido Cavalcanti. Most annotated editions of the
Vita Nuova give this reply by Cavalcanti to the first sonnet. It begins:
Vedeste al mio parere onne valore.

Page 14

The significant detail. The prose of chapter III reads:

> Appresso ciò poco dimorava che la sua letizia si convertia in amarissimo
> pianto; e così piangendo, si ricogliea questa donna ne le sue braccia, e con
> essa mi parea che si ne gisse *verso lo cielo.*

The sonnet, however, ends as follows:

> poi la svegliava, e d'esto core ardendo
> lei paventosa umilmente pascea:
> appresso gir lo ne vedea piangendo.

Page 14

The distinguishing mark. The passages which state in each case
the awareness of the protagonist at the time of the presence of a number
nine are these:

> Chapter III (first vision): . . . onde io sostenea sì grande angoscia che
> lo mio deboletto sonno non poteo sostenere, anzi si ruppe e fui disvegliato. E
> mantenente cominciai a pensare, e trovai che l'ora ne la quale m'era questa
> visione apparita era la quarta de la notte stata; sì che appare manifestamente
> ch'ella fue la prima ora de le nove ultime ore de la notte.

Chapter xII (second vision): E dette queste parole, sì disparve, e lo mio sonno fue rotto. Onde io ricordandomi trovai che questa visione m'era apparita ne la nona ora del die.

Chapter xxIII (third vision): Appresso ciò per pochi dì avvenne che in alcuna parte de la mia persona mi giunse una dolorosa infermitade, onde io continuamente soffersi per nove dì amarissima pena; la quale mi condusse a tanta debolezza, che me convenia stare come coloro li quali non si possono muovere. Io dico che ne lo nono giorno, sentendome dolere quasi intollerabilemente, a me giunse un pensero. . .

And the third vision develops out of that thought.

Page 14

"Daydreams." See the appearance of the God of Love in chapter IX:

E però lo dolcissimo segnore, lo quale mi segnoreggiava per la vertù de la gentilissima donna ne la mia imaginazione apparve come peregrino leggeramente vestito e di vili drappi.

And see the God's disappearance in the same chapter:

E dette queste parole, disparve questa mia imaginazione tutta subitamente per la grandissima parte che mi parve che Amore mi desse di sè.

It should be noted that, in connection with the third vision, when there is a reason for withholding the name of *visione,* it is precisely the term *imaginazione* that is used: *Appresso questa vana imaginazione* (chapter xxIV); and again (*ivi*): *dopo la imaginazione del suo fedele.*

The appearance of the God again in chapter xxIV is another *imaginazione:*

Allora dico che mi giunse una imaginazione d'Amore; che mi parve vederlo venire da quella parte ove la mia donna stava e pareami che lietamente mi dicesse nel cor mio. . .

An *imaginazione* is strongly subjective. A *visione* is something much more objective and, being prophetic, also, in some sense, more real.

Page 15

Love's answer to the poet's question. For a more detailed examination and interpretation of chapter xII of the *Vita Nuova,* and the so-called obscure words pronounced by the God of Love, (*Ego tanquam centrum circuli,* etc.), I refer the reader to my article, *"Vita Nuova XII: Love's Obscure Words,"* in the *Romanic Review* (1945), pp. 89-102.

For the shift from Latin to Italian, see a note on "The Use of Latin in the *Vita Nuova*," *Modern Language Notes*, LXI, pp. 108-112. J. E. Shaw, in his *Essays on the Vita Nuova* (Princeton University Press, 1929), devotes an essay to this point and gives a summary of the various interpretations that have been made of the meaning of Love's words (pp. 77-108). Only recently Professor Shaw has expressed his disagreement with my own views (*Italica*, XXIV, 113-118). I am glad that now, with this essay, my distinguished colleague can know what my view of the whole of the *Vita Nuova* is, and can see all of the reasons for arriving at the conclusions expressed in my articles.

Pages 16-17

The figure of the circle and the center of the circle. See my article in the *Romanic Review* cited above. Two well-known *dantisti*, M. Barbi and G. Boffito, had already seen that Love's words, in expressing that figure, point to the attribute of omniscience in the Deity; and F. Beck had made an extensive study of the use of the figure throughout the centuries ("Die rätselhaften Worte in Dantes *Vita Nuova*," *Zeitschrift für romanische Philologie* [1927], pp. 1-27), from which study the traditional use of the figure in this regard is clear. But neither should the verses of *Paradiso*, xvii, 13-18, be forgotten in this connection, where Dante speaks to Cacciaguida as follows:

> O cara piota mia che sì t'insusi,
>   che come veggion le terrene menti
>   non capere in triangol due ottusi,
>
> così vedi le cose contingenti
>   anzi che sieno in sè, mirando *il punto*
>   *a cui tutti li tempi son presenti.*

Of course, to say that the God of Love *foresees* the future is merely to state the case from the human point of view. To see, moreover, that an attribute of the Christian Deity has here been accorded to the God of Love demands no more of any reader than what the reading of poetry usually demands.

Page 19

The delirious dream. Thomas Aquinas (*Summa theologica*, II-II, 95, 6 ad Resp.), in discussing the causes of dreams, distinguishes between the corporeal and the spiritual cause, and has this to say of the former:

Quandoque vero causa intrinseca somniorum est corporalis: nam ex interiori dispositione corporis formatur aliquis motus in phantasia conveniens tali dispositione; sicut homini in quo abundant frigidi humores, occurrunt insomnia quod sit in aqua vel nive; et propter hoc medici dicunt esse intendendum somniis ad cognoscendum interiores dispositiones.

The protagonist of the *Vita Nuova* thought at the time that his dream had a corporeal cause. Only *post eventum* was he to realize that it was "true."

Page 19

The visionary death of Beatrice like an ascension. One should compare the miraculous death of Galahad which Mme Lot-Borodine has described as follows (*Trois Essais sur le roman de Lancelot du Lac et la quête du saint Graal* [Paris, 1921], p. 119):

Après un émouvant adieu à ses deux compagnons, Galaad, étendu en croix devant le Graal, expire. C'est moins une mort qu'une Assomption. Pendant qu'une troupe d'anges emporte son âme "en compagnie de Jhesu Crist" une main, descendant des cieux, saisit le saint vaisseau et la lance et les soustrait pour toujours aux regards mortels. Le cercle mystique se ferme. Tout est accompli. Et le neuvième fleuve se jette enfin dans l'Océan de lumière.

Page 20

Beatrice's death like the death of Christ. Many readers have, of course, recognized the obvious resemblance—none, I think, more clearly than A. Marigo (*Mistica e scienza nella Vita Nuova* [Padova, 1914], pp. 45-46):

La natura si commuove tutta: "pareami vedere lo sole oscurare sì che le stelle si mostravano di colore ch'elle mi faceano giudicare che piangessero" (Gerem. IV, 28: *lugebit terra et moerebunt coeli desuper*) . . . I segni terribili sembrano quelli che nell'Apocalissi VI, 12, preannunziano la fine del mondo: *et ecce terraemotus magnus factus est et sol factus est niger.* Pari sconvolgimento del creato non leggiamo essere avvenuto che per la morte di Cristo (Matt. XXIV).

For further discussion of the particular signs (the earthquake, the stars weeping, and so forth) and their mention elsewhere, see E. Proto, "Beatrice beata," *Giornale dantesco,* XIV, 66ff.

Cf. *Paradiso,* xxvii, 34-36:

Così Beatrice trasmutò sembianza;
e tale eclissi credo che'n ciel fue
quando patì la suprema possanza.

See also *Paradiso,* xxix, 97-102.

Page 22

The figure in white raiment. J. E. Shaw (*Essays on the Vita Nuova,*
p. 84) has remarked the resemblance:

One cannot help being reminded of that other youth 'clothed in white
raiment' who appeared to Mary Magdalen and the others in the holy sepulchre.
In the *Convivio* Dante interprets the latter angel as representing 'nobility' . . .
and since, in this passage of the *Vita Nuova* Dante addressed Love . . . as
'Segnore de la nobilitade' we may reasonably suppose that both figures were
suggested by the angel of the sepulchre.

One might, I think, note another passage in Scriptures which, in
view of the connection of the number nine, may have some part in the
cluster of associations here (Actus. Apost. [Vulg.] X, 30):

A nudiusquarta die usque hanc horam, orans eram hora nona in domo
mea, et ecce vir stetit ante me in veste candida.

Page 23

The death of Christ in the ninth hour. Some reader might object
that, according to a passage in the *Convivio* (IV, xxiii, 92-110), it was
the sixth hour when Christ died:

E ciò manifesta l'ora del giorno de la sua morte, [Christ's death] che volle
quella consimigliare con la vita sua; onde dice Luca che era quasi ora sesta
quando morio che è a dire lo colmo del die.

But, as the editors of the *Convivio* (Busnelli and Vandelli [Florence,
1937], II, 297-298) observe, apropos of this passage:

Va però qui osservato che Dante, affermando che Cristo morì quasi all'ora
sesta, al colmo del sole, intende dire che, per farlo morire, allora fu crocifisso:
Cristo morì tre ore dopo.

See also E. Moore, *Studies in Dante,* I, 89-90; *Inferno,* xxi, 112-114.
In Guillaume Durand, *Rationale divinorum officiorum* (Venice, 1589),
fol. 59v, one reads:

Celebratur autem missa hora tertia, sexta et nona. . . In sexta, quia illa
hora (secundum Matthaeum) vere crucifixus et immolatus est. Et in nona,
quia illa hora in cruce pendens emisit spiritum.

Moreover, the importance of the number nine in connection with the
death of Christ is apparent at a point a little further on in the *Convivio*
(IV, xxiv, 6):

> Onde avemo di Platone, del quale ottimamente si può dire che fosse
> naturato e per la sua perfezione e per la fisonomia che di lui prese Socrate
> quando prima lo vide, che esso vivette ottantuno anno, secondo che testimonia
> Tullio in quello De Senectute. E io credo che se Cristo fosse stato non cruci-
> fisso, e fosse vivuto lo spazio che la sua vita poteva secondo natura trapassare,
> elli sarebbe a li ottantuno anno di mortale corpo in eternale transmutato.

That the significance of the number eighty-one lies in the fact that
it is the product of nine times nine is evident from a well-known passage
in Seneca (*Epistulae morales,* edited by Hense [Lipsiae, 1898], III, 173
[no. VI (58)]):

> Nam hoc scis, puto, Platoni diligentiae suae beneficio contigisse quod
> natali suo decessit, et annum unum atque octogesimum implevit, sine ulla
> deductione. Ideo Magi, qui forte Athenis erant, immolaverunt defuncto,
> amplioris fuisse sortis quam humanae rati, quia consummasset perfectissimum
> numerum quem novem novies multiplicata componunt.

Page 23

The princes of the earth. Vita Nuova, chapter xxx:

> Poi che fue partita da questo secolo, rimase tutta la sopradetta cittade
> quasi vedova dispogliata da ogni dignitade; onde io, ancora lagrimando in
> questa desolata cittade, *scrissi a li principi de la terra* alquanto de la sua
> condizione, pigliando quello cominciamento di Geremia profeta che dice:
> *Quomodo sedet sola civitas.*

Those interpreters who are ever ready to reduce the *Vita Nuova* to
something more in keeping with the prosaic and "real" world which
they themselves inhabit have wanted the phrase to mean "principal men
of the city" instead of "princes of the earth" (see M. Scherillo, *Alcuni
capitoli della biografia di Dante* [Torino, 1896], pp. 375-395). But one
may simply compare the words of Guido da Montefeltro in *Inferno,*
xxvii, 76-78:

> Li accorgimenti e le coperte vie
>   io seppi tutte, e sì menai lor arte,
>   ch'al fine de la terra il suono uscie.

The expression there, as Vandelli, among others, notes, is modeled on that of Psalms (Vulg.) XVIII, 4: *In omnem terram exivit sonus eorum; et in fines terrae verba eorum.*

Page 23

Let these sayings . . . (Luke IX, 44-45). There are, of course, several other passages so appropriate in this respect that it is hard to choose the best among them:

John (Vulg.) XII, 14ff.: Et invenit Jesus asellum et sedit super eum, sicut scriptum est: Noli timere filia Sion; ecce rex tuus venit sedens super pullum asinae. Haec non cognoverunt discipuli eius primum; *sed quando glorificatus est Jesus,* tunc recordati sunt quia haec erant scripta de eo et haec fecerunt ei.

John (Vulg.) XIII, 7: Quod ego facio, tu nescis modo, scies autem postea.

See also John XII, 32; II, 18-22; Mark IX, 31; Augustine, *Enarratio in Psalmum XLV, PL* 36, 518, gloss to v. 4.

Quid jam sequitur ex eo quod translati sunt montes in cor maris? Attendite et videte veritatem. Haec enim quando dicebantur, obscura erant, quia nondum contigerant: nunc autem quis iam facta non cognoscat?

With this compare what is said of the true meaning of the first vision in the *Vita Nuova* at the end of chapter III:

Lo verace guidicio del detto sogno non fue veduto allora per alcuno, ma ora è manifestissimo a li più semplici.

Page 24

The death of Our Lord Jesus Christ standing at the center of the universe. One may recall those medieval maps which show Jerusalem as the center of the hemisphere of land, that center indicated by Christ on the Cross (see the famous Hereford Map). Cf. also the following passage in E. Gilson, *La Philosophie de s. Bonaventure* (Paris, 1924), p. 381, giving the Saint's thought on this point:

Le verbe est devenu le centre de l'univers en se faisant chair et en habitant parmi nous. Ce qu'il est dans l'Incarnation, il l'est encore dans sa Passion, car c'est lui qui restaure l'oeuvre de création détruite par la faute de l'homme. Nous savons *qu'il est aussi le milieu par où l'âme rejoint Dieu dans l'extase de cette vie* et le théologien pourrait montrer sans peine qu'il est encore le moyen de la béatification eternelle: *Agnus in medio aquarum est Filius Dei, Filius dico, qui est media persona a qua omnis beatitudo* (*In Hexaëm* I, 38. t. V, p. 335).

See also Psalms (Vulg.) LXXIII, 12: *Operatus est salutem in medio terrae.*

The student of the *Divine Comedy* will remember, moreover, that the whole Rose of *Paradiso* is divided according to the same principle (*Paradiso,* xxxii, 22ff.):

> Da questa parte onde'l fiore è maturo
> di tutte le sue foglie, sono assisi
> quei che credettero in Cristo venturo;
>
> dall'altra parte onde sono intercisi
> di voti i semicirculi, si stanno
> quei ch'a Cristo venuto ebber li visi.

And, at the end of time, the petals on the one side will equal in number those on the other:

> Or mira l'alto proveder divino;
> che l'uno e l'altro aspetto della fede
> igualmente empierà questo giardino.

Page 26

The Book of Memory. The metaphor is an old one and in no way original with Dante. But neither are we to assume that Dante got it from a diplomatic letter of Piero delle Vigne, as Zingarelli (*Bollettino della società dantesca italiana,* I, 98-101) has claimed. That Piero's phrase "in tenaci memoriae libro perlegimus" should have suggested not only the opening metaphor of the *Vita Nuova* but all the other instances of the metaphor in the *Divine Comedy* as well is simply one of those fantastic claims of "influence" with which Dante scholarship (and not only Dante scholarship!) is unfortunately so replete. (See *Inferno,* ii, 8; xv, 88; *Paradiso,* xvii, 91ff.; xxiii, 54; also Dante's *canzone* beginning *E' m'incresce di me sì duramente,* vs. 57ff.) For the image and metaphor of the "book" (not only the "book of memory") in the *Divine Comedy,* see E. R. Curtius, "Das Buch als Symbol in der Divina Commedia," *Festschrift Paul Clemen* (Bonn, 1926), pp. 44-54.

I am unable to say what the first instance of the metaphor "book of memory" is. But that the metaphor is an established one in Dante's time the following passages leave, I think, no doubt: Hugh of St. Victor, *Explanatio in canticum beatae Mariae,* in *PL* 175, 430, glossing the text *Fecit potentiam in brachio suo; dispersit superbos mente cordis sui:*

Et si aliam adhuc expositionem accommodare velimus, erit non contemnenda sententia. Mens etenim cordis Dei est vivax illa, et permanens dispositio internae occultaeque praedestinationis. Ipse est liber vitae in quo scripta sunt nomina eorum qui salvi fiunt et scripti in vita in Hierusalem. Idem ergo mens est quod liber, et quasi in libro scribitur, quod in mente per memoriam retentum non deletur. Quod itaque in hoc loco dictum est: Dispersit superbos mente cordis sui, hoc idem Psalmista aliis verbis expressit, dicens: Deleantur de libro viventium (Psal. LXVIII).

Certainly in Christian thought the image of a book of memory is closely connected with that of the book of life, as is evident from a passage in Augustine which is, in itself, enough to establish the connection between the two: *De civitate Dei,* XX, xiv, commenting on Revelation XX, 12:

Non ergo unus liber erit omnium sed singuli singulorum. Scriptura vero ista unum volens intelligi, *Et alius,* inquit, *liber apertus est.* Quaedam igitur vis est intelligenda divina, qua fiet ut cuique opera sua, vel bona vel mala cuncta in memoriam revocentur, et mentis intuiti mira celeritate cernantur; ut accuset, vel excuset scientia conscientiam; atque ita simul et omnes et singuli judicentur. Quae nimirum vis divina, libri nomen accepit. In ea quippe quodammodo legitur, quidquid ea faciente recolitur.

See also Augustine, *In canticum Magnificat,* vol. VI of his works in *PL,* col. 1660:

Mens etiam cordis Dei est vivax et permanens dispositio aeternae occultaeque praedestinationis. Ipse est liber vitae. Idem est ergo mens, quod liber.

One of the best witnesses to the currency of the metaphor in later times and in connection with the Book of Life is the following in Alanus de Insulis, *Liber in distinctionibus,* etc., s. v. *liber* (*PL* 210, 837):

Quandoque est substantivum et dicitur similitudo libri, unde legitur quod Dominus ostendit Ezechieli librum grandem in quo erant scripta carmina, lamentationes et vae, et similitudo libri. Dicitur memoria, unde in Apoc.: Scribe hoc in libro, id est, commenda hoc memoria. Dicitur divina praedestinatio, unde Moyses: Aut dele me de libro vitae, aut dimitte eis hanc noxam . . . et alibi in Psalmo: Et in libro tuo omnes scribentur. Dicitur conscientia unde *Dan.* Sedit plenus dierum et libri aperti sunt coram eo, quia in judicio singulorum conscientia patebit.

Note also, *ivi* s. v. *mens:*

anima. . . Dicitur memoria, unde in *Apoc.* In mente ergo habe qualiter acceperis.

See also Aquinas, *Summa theologica,* I, 24, 1, where the above passage from Augustine is cited and glossed.

Page 27

The scribe. A student of the *Divine Comedy* will recall the following verses of *Paradiso,* x, 25-27:

> Messo t'ho innanzi: omai per te ti ciba;
> chè a sè torce tutta la mia cura
> *quella materia ond'io son fatto scriba.*

Page 28

Sentenzia. For the meaning of this word here, one may compare an analogous passage in the *Convivio* (I, ɪ, 110), where, as here, the author is stating his intention in the work which is to follow:

> Ma questo pane, cioè la presente sposizione, sarà la luce, la quale ogni colore di loro sentenzia [that is, of the *canzoni* to be explained] farà parvente.

See also *ivi,* I, ɪx, 7.

I have translated as "substance," but that word does not cover all the meaning of *sentenzia* unless it be allowed to include also that of "intention" or "intended meaning," as may be seen from a passage in *Paradiso,* ɪv, 49ff:

> Quel che Timeo dell'anime argomenta
> non è simile a ciò che qui si vede,
> però che, come dice, par che senta.

> Dice che l'alma alla sua stella riede,
> credendo quella quindi esser decisa
> quando natura per forma la diede;

> e forse sua sentenza è d'altra guisa
> che la voce non suona, ed esser puote
> con intenzion da non esser derisa.

But perhaps the clearest example of all is in the *Vita Nuova* itself (chapter xxxɪx):

> Onde io, volendo che cotale desiderio malvagio e vana tentazione paresse distrutto, sì che alcuno dubbio non potessero inducere le rimate parole ch'io avea dette innanzi, propuosi di fare uno sonetto ne lo quale io comprendesse la sentenzia di questa ragione.

E. Auerbach, "Passio als Leidenschaft," *Publications of the Modern Language Association* (1941), p. 1181, remarks on the Latin form as follows:

Gibt es ja doch auch im Lateinischen kein entsprechendes Wort für "Gedanke." *Cogitatio* seit Cicero belegt, deckt unser Bedeutungsfeld "Gedanke" ebenso wenig wie *sensus* des Feld "Gefühl." Ja, man kann ein von *sentire* abgeleitetes Wort, *sententia,* zuweilen für "Gedanke" verwenden, und "Platos Gedanken über das Schöne" lässt sich gut wiedergeben durch *quid Plato de pulchro senserit.*

Page 30

A long polemic. A comprehensive account of this controversy is to be found in Shaw, *Essays on the Vita Nuova,* pp. 163ff: "The Character of the *Vita Nuova,*" with relevant bibliography in the notes at the end of this chapter.

Page 31

The poet unable to remember anything about Beatrice's death. This is the interpretation of Shaw, *Essays on the Vita Nuova,* p. 151:

I conclude therefore that the first reason given by Dante, in Chapter XXVIII (XXIX) for not presenting the usual poem and commentary—namely that such a "trattato" would not be "del presente proposito," according to the statement in the "proemio"—means that he had no memory of the circumstances of the death of Beatrice, and that, owing to the suddenness and shocking character of the event, he had no memory of his own feelings on becoming aware of it.

Page 33

The "digression." The student of the *Convivio* and the *De vulgari eloquentia* will recall that some such phrase as *tornando al proposito* is not uncommon in those works:

Convivio, III, x, 1: Partendomi da questa digressione, che mestiere è stata a vedere la veritade, ritorno al proposito e dico.

IV, ıv, 14: Ma però che in questo capitolo sanza troppa lunghezza ciò trattare non si potrebbe, e li lunghi capitoli sono inimici de la memoria, farò ancora digressione d'altro capitolo per le toccate ragioni mostrare.

De vulgari eloquentia, I, vı, 4: . . . redeuntes igitur ad propositum.

I, xii, 6: Sed prestat ad propositum repedare quam. . .

II, i, 1: . . . et ad calamum frugi operis redeuntes.

But such instances find their explanation within their respective contexts, as that of the *Vita Nuova* does within the figure of a Book of Memory being copied by a scribe whose declared *proposito* is to copy.

Page 36

A touch of shame. One feels this reflected, for instance, in the word *almanaccamento* used by Barbi in speaking of chapter xxix (*Bollettino della società dantesca italiana,* VIII, 265):

> E il fatto che nella canzone che segue *Gli occhi dolenti* il poeta non tralascia di dar i particolari della morte di Beatrice, ci deve far credere che Dante pensasse piuttosto ad entrare nel c. XXVIII in sottili considerazioni sulla ragione della partita della sua donna e quindi sulla sua missione in terra e sulla sua condizione privilegiata in cielo (cosa pure estranea al suo proposito): di fatti volendo pur dirne qualche cosa, fa seguire quell'almanaccamento sul tre e sul nove che finisce col proclamare Beatrice un miracolo la cui radice è la divina Trinità, almanaccamento che non può dirsi certamente un ricordo del libro della memoria del poeta.

Page 38

Galileo, Browne. For the figure in Galileo, see *Frammenti e lettere,* con introd. e note di G. Gentile (Livorno, 1917), p. 4: . . . "volgersi al gran libro della natura." Gentile here notes several other occurrences of it.

Browne's *Religio Medici,* part I, section 16: "Thus there are two books from whence I collect my divinity; besides that written one of God, another of his servant Nature, that universal and publick manuscript, that lies expans'd unto the eyes of all: those that never saw him in the one have discovered him in the other."

Cf. also Raymond Sebon, *La Théologie naturelle,* translated by Montaigne (Paris, 1932), author's preface, p. ix:

> Dieu nous a donné deux livres, celuy de l'universel ordre des choses ou de la nature, et celuy de la Bible. Cestuy-là nous fut donné premier, et dès l'origine du monde: car chaque creature n'est que comme une lettre, tirée per la main de Dieu. De façon que d'une grande multitude de créatures, comme d'un nombre de lettres, ce livre a été composé: dans lequel l'homme se trouve, et en est la lettre capitale et principale.

See also T. Campanella's sonnet beginning

Il mondo è un libro dove il Senno eterno
scrisse i propri concetti

in the volume Campanella, *Poesie,* a cura di G. Gentile (Firenze, 1939), p. 30, where Gentile notes:

Il concetto che il mondo sia libro di Dio, ricorre frequentissimamente nel Campanella. . . Si veda p.e. il proemio della *Metaph.,* p. 2: "Deus autem duobus ad nos loquitur viis, nempe vel res ipsas producendo vel revelando humano more, sicut doctor discipulis. Cum Deus res facit, codicem vivum facit vel auget, in quo dispicientes addiscamus. Unde dictum est . . . quod universitas rerum quam Mundum appellamus, olim sapientia Dei vocata est; et S. Antonius et Bernardus et Chrysostomus Mundum vocant Dei Codicem; et profecto sic est, quoniam hic Deus scribit omnes conceptus suos et verbo ipsum exprimit.

Pages 38-39

Hugh of St. Victor, *Eruditionis didascalicae liber septimus, PL* 176, 814. For the concept expressed by Hugh with the words "et singulae creaturae quasi figurae quaedam sunt non humano placito inventae sed divino arbitrio institutae," all important for the way in which the Book of Memory is read by its scribe, one may compare what Augustine says of the validity of logical sequence (*De doctrina christiana,* II, 32, *PL* 34, 58):

Ipsa tamen veritas connexionum non instituta, sed animadversa est ab hominibus et notata, ut eam possint vel discere vel docere: nam est in rerum ratione perpetua et divinitus instituta. Sicut enim qui narrat ordinem temporum, non eum ipse componit; et locorum situs, aut naturas animalium vel stirpium vel lapidum qui ostendit, non res ostendit ab hominibus institutas.

Page 39

St. Bonaventura, *Breviloquium,* pars II, 11. On this notion in the Saint's philosophy, see Gilson, *La Philosophie de s. Bonaventure,* p. 419. See also Hugh of St. Victor, *PL* 176, 266.

Ezechiel (Vulg.) II, 9-10: Et vidi: et ecce manus missa ad me, in qua erat involutus liber; et expandit illum coram me, qui erat scriptus intus et foris.

Page 40

Thomas Aquinas, *Summa theologica,* I, 1, 10 ad Resp.:

Auctor sacrae Scripturae est Deus, in cuius potestate est ut non solum voces ad significandum accommodet (quod etiam homo facere potest) sed etiam res ipsas. Et ideo, cum in omnibus scientiis voces significent, hoc habet proprium ista scientia, quod ipsae res significatae per voces, etiam significant aliquid. Illa ergo prima significatio qua voces significant res, pertinet ad primum sensum, qui est sensus historicus vel litteralis. Illa vero significatio qua res significatae per voces, iterum res alias significant, dicitur sensus spiritualis; qui super litteralem fundatur, et eum supponit.

The translation of this passage in the text is from *The "Summa Theologica" of St. Thomas Aquinas,* translated by Fathers of the English Dominican Province (London, n. d.), I, 17.

See also St. Bonaventura, *Breviloquium,* Proemium 5:

Quoniam autem Deus non tantum loquitur per verba, verum etiam per facta, quia ipsius dicere facere est, et ipsius facere dicere.

Page 41

Augustine, *De doctrina christiana,* II, 28 (*PL* 34, 56):

Narratione autem historica cum praeterita etiam hominum instituta narrantur, non inter humana instituta ipsa historia numeranda est; quia jam quae transierunt, nec infecta fieri possunt, in ordine temporum habenda sunt, quorum est conditor et administrator Deus.

The translation of this passage in the text is that of J. F. Shaw in *A Select Library of the Nicene and Post-Nicene Fathers of the Christian Church,* First Series, II (Buffalo, 1887), 549.

See also the method of Dante's reasoning in his own *De monarchia,* where he scrutinizes history for the visible signs of God's will; and especially II, ii, 8:

Voluntas quidem Dei per se invisibilis est; sed "invisibilia Dei per ea que facta sunt intellecta conspiciuntur"; nam occulto existente sigillo, cera impressa de illo quamvis occulto tradit notitiam manifestam. Nec mirum si divina voluntas per signa querenda est, cum etiam humana extra volentem non aliter quam per signa cernatur.

Page 41

Augustine, *De doctrina christiana,* II, 40.

Page 41

No human eye will ever see all the meaning. See St. Bonaventura, *In Hexaëmeron,* XIII, 2 (Quaracchi edition, t.V, p. 388):

Quis potest scire infinitatem seminum, cum tamen in uno sint silvae silvarum et postea infinita semina? Sic ex scripturis elici possunt infinitae theoriae, quas nullus potest comprehendere nisi solus Deus.

Pages 41-42

Augustine on the Exodus. Shaw's translation of *On Christian Doctrine* in *Nicene and Post-Nicene Fathers,* pp. 554-555.

Page 42

On the symbolism and interpretation of numbers, which played an important part in the writing of the later Neoplatonists (cf. Inge, *Plotinus,* I, 110), see Augustine, *De trinitate,* IV, 4; Hugh of St. Victor, *De Scripturis et Scripturis sacris, PL,* 175, 21-22; also, E. Mâle, *L'Art religieux du XIIIe siècle en France* (3rd ed., Paris, 1900), pp. 23ff.

Pages 43-44

The divisions. Far too much has been made of specific sources for the *divisioni* of the *Vita Nuova.* It was not necessary for Dante to take the suggestion of them from any one work or writer. The procedure which they represent is, of course, very common. See, for example, St. Bonaventura's *Commentary on the Sentences of Peter Lombard.* I choose the following at random (II, 11-14, of the Quaracchi edition of the *Opera omnia*):

Unde liber iste secundus, qui incipit: *Creationem rerum,* etc., dividitur in duas partes. In prima agit de hominis conditione; in secunda de lapsu eius et tentatione, infra distinctione vigesima prima: *videns igitur diabolus,* etc.

Prima pars habet duas. In prima determinat de conditione rerum quantum ad principium efficiens, in secunda vero quantum ad finem, ibi: *Et quia non valet eius beautitudinis,* etc. Prima pars habet tres particulas. . .

Page 46

Boccaccio's "edition" of the Vita Nuova. For all details on his omission of the *divisioni* or his relegating them to the margins of his copy, and his reasons for this, see M. Barbi's critical edition of the *Vita Nuova,* p. xvi.

Page 46

The world as a work of art. See Etienne Gilson, *L'Esprit de la philosophie médiévale* (Paris, 1944), p. 372:

A la suite de saint Augustin, le moyen âge se représentait donc l'histoire du monde comme un beau poème, dont le sens est pour nous intelligible et complet depuis que nous en connaissons le commencement et la fin. Sans doute, en bien de ses parties, le sens caché du poème nous échappe; on dirait que l'"ineffable musicien" a voulu garder pour lui son secret; pourtant, nous en déchiffrons assez pour être sûrs que tout a un sens et conjecturer le rapport de chaque événement à la loi unique qui en règle la composition tout entière.

Page 47

A faculty capable of digesting the sensible in terms of a rational understanding. See Gilson, *L'Esprit de la philosophie médiévale,* p. 258.

En premier lieu, on voudra bien noter [in the philosophy of Thomas Aquinas] que, si débile qu'il soit, l'intellect humain est et reste un intellect, c'est-à-dire, une capacité de devenir en quelque sorte toute chose par mode de représentation. C'est sa misère que de ne pouvoir assimiler que l'intelligible inclus dans le sensible, mais ce qu'il y cherche, c'est precisément l'intelligible, et rien ne l'arrêtra dans cette quête, tant qu'il lui restera de l'intelligible à assimiler.

The concept of the intelligible enclosed in the sensible is fundamental for medieval exegesis and aesthetic. It accounts not only for the idea of *aprire* in the act of rendering the word intelligible, but that expressed by *enucleare* as well: for this, see again Augustine, *De doctrina christiana, PL* 34, 73:

Tota figurata sunt: quorum ad charitatis pastum enucleanda secreta sunt.

For further repercussions of the doctrine in medieval literature, see Leo Spitzer in *Zeitschrift für romanische Philologie* LIV, 237, and *Modern Philology,* XLI, 97. Compare in the same connection Dante's *De monarchia,* II, chap. i:

Sed postquam medullitus oculos mentis infixi et per efficacissima signa divinam providentiam hox effecisse cognovi.

Page 47

In a similar spirit the gloss to Holy Scripture sought to "open up" the meaning of the words of God. See Augustine at the beginning of *De doctrina christiana* (*PL* 34, 15):

Sunt praecepta quaedam tractandarum Scripturarum quae studiosis earum video non incommode posse tradi; ut non solum legendo alios qui divinarum Litterarum *operta aperuerunt,* sed et aliis ipsi aperiendo proficiant.

And *ivi,* col. 18:

. . . seditque cum eo Philippus, qui noverat Isaiam prophetam, eique humanis verbis et lingua quod in Scriptura illa tectum erat, aperuit (*Act.* VIII, 27-38).

And again, *ivi,* col. 84:

Tichonius . . . facit librum quem Regularum vocavit, quia in eo quasdam septem regulas exsecutus est, quibus quasi clavibus divinarum Scripturarum aperirentur occulta.

Page 50

Poems like the creation, poets like God. Of course, poets may simply hide their reasons in their work so that the discovery of them may be more exciting. Compare on this point Petrarch, *Africa,* IX, 90:

Accipe quam brevibus. Non illa licentia vatum est
quam multis placuisse palam est.
Scripturum iecisse prius firmissima veri
fundamenta decet, quibus inde innixus amoena
et varia sub nube potest abscondere sese,
lectori longum cumulans placidumque laborem,
quaesitu asperior quo sit sententia, verum
dulcior inventu.

Page 51

Poems have their causes in the real world. It is for the poet to distinguish them as worthy causes, however. Cf. *Vita Nuova,* xxii:

Onde io poi, pensando, propuosi di dire parole, *acciò che degnamente avea cagione di dire,* ne le quali parole io conchiudesse tutto ciò che inteso avea da queste donne.

Or the poet may take his *matera* from something which *might have been* in the real world, as may be seen in the words which continue the above:

E però che volentieri l'averei domandate, se non mi fosse stata riprensione, presi tanta matera di dire come s'io l'avesse domandate ed elle m'avessero risposto.

Page 51

Ragione. For the Provençal *razos* see A. Jenroy, *La Poésie lyrique des troubadours* (Paris, 1934), I, 101ff.:

Les *razos* sont de brèves notices relatives non au sens de certaines pièces, mais aux circonstances d'où elles seraient nées et aux personnages qui y figurent.

Le mot [razo] signifie proprement "explication" "commentaire" (de razonar: "expliquer").

Dans les manuscrits les plus anciens, les Biographies sont placées en tête des oeuvres de chaque poète, les "razos" en tête des pièces qu'elles concernent.

In short, the Provençal *razo* is quite obviously a *ragionata cagione.* Many scholars have variously discussed the matter of a historical connection between the *ragioni* of the *Vita Nuova* and the Provençal *razos:* P. Rajna, *Lo schema della Vita Nuova* (Verona, 1890); V. Crescini, "Les razos provenzali e le prose della *Vita Nuova,*" *Giornale storico della letteratura italiana,* XXXII, 463 ff.; Tobler, in *Archiv für das Studium der neueren Sprachen,* LXXXV, 121. But here, as in the case of the *divisioni,* scholars have too much wanted a specific source for Dante's *ragioni.* There is no specific source. The metaphor of a Book of Memory has no such source, the *divisioni* have no such source, the *ragioni* have no such source. All three are one cluster of metaphor around a way of looking at the world which was common and familiar to Dante's age.

Such a cluster here does not mean, obviously, that the *ragioni* may appear only in connection with the other two. There is no "book of memory" and there are no *divisioni* in the Provençal manuscripts. Neither does the *Convivio* use the image of a Book of Memory; and yet the *Convivio* speaks more than once of a *ragionata cagione* and of *divisioni,* and has, of course, the appearance of a book of poems glossed in prose (XXX, xii, 1):

Nel primo capitolo di questo trattato è sì compiutamente *ragionata la cagione* che mosse me a questa canzone, che non è più mestiere di ragionare, che assai leggermente a questa esposizione ch'è detta ella si può riducere. E però secondo *le divisioni fatte* la litterale sentenza trascorrerò, per questa volgendo lo senso de la lettera là dove sarà mestiere.

And see *passim* for many examples of *ragionare* in the identical sense it has in the *Vita Nuova.*

But it does mean that, given the image of a Book of Memory, the idea of gloss implicit in both the *ragione* and the *divisione* is the more naturally present. I mean not only that the idea of Book brings this about, but the idea of Memory as well. In St. Augustine's philosophy, the memory is a place of understanding (see note to p. 115 further on). This notion of memory becomes through his philosophy an accepted one. See, for example, St. Bonaventura, *Itinerarium mentis in Deum,* chap. iii, at the beginning:

> Intra igitur ad te, et vide, quoniam mens tua amat ferventissime semetipsam, nec se posset amare nisi se nosceret, ne se nosceret nisi se meminisset *quia nihil capimus* per intelligentiam quod non sit *praesens apud nostram memoriam.* Et ex hoc advertis animam tuam triplicem habere potentiam, non oculo carnis sed oculo rationis.

The *ragioni* and the *divisioni* in the Book of Memory are precisely such a turning of the eye of reason back over what is said or done and is now held fixed in the memory before the eye of the mind. See, for instance, the method of St. Bonaventura in his *Breviloquium* where, having set forth a statement of doctrine he begins a paragraph, "Ratio autem ad intelligentiam praedictorum haec est."

The *ragioni* and the *divisioni* and the Book of Memory have roots deep in the medieval mind.

Page 53

The multiple gloss. For the gloss to Holy Scriptures, see B. Smalley, *The Study of the Bible in the Middle Ages* (Oxford, 1941). Also, for the idea of glossing in general, *ivi,* pp. 31ff.:

> In the Middle Ages both teaching and original thinking centered in texts which had been handed down from an earlier period, whether it were an inspired text, the Bible, or a *corpus iuris,* or a classical author. Hence it [a gloss] was essential for teaching purposes. We find this development both in biblical study and in Roman and canon law. All three produced a *Glossa ordinaria.*

And p. 37:

> These references and most of the glosses proper were written in the margin of the text, but some of the shorter glosses were written between the lines simply to save space.

And for glossing the gloss, see p. 43.

For manuscripts of Vergil with multiple gloss see J. J. H. Savage, "The Manuscripts of the Commentary of Servius Danielis on Virgil," *Harvard Studies in Classical Philology,* XLIII (1932), 77ff.

Page 57

Beatrice as Love. The identity (in metaphor) of the God and Beatrice is, in fact, already clear in the sonnet of chapter VIII:

> Audite quanto Amor le fece orranza,
> ch'io'l vidi lamentare in forma vera
> sovra la morta imagine avvenente;
> e riguardava ver lo ciel sovente,

where it is clear, according to the prose, that *Amor in forma vera* was Beatrice.

Page 60

The signs of the tradition. Cf. L. F. Mott, *The System of Courtly Love studied as an Introduction to the Vita Nuova of Dante* (Boston, 1896). But surely it is time now that another monograph should gather together all of the results of the many scattered studies on the tradition of courtly love made since 1896 and bring to bear on the subject that increased understanding of the tradition which has resulted from them.

Page 61

Love moves the universe. Cf. P. Rousselot, *Pour l'histoire du problème de l'amour au moyen âge* (Beiträge zur Geschichte der Philosophie des Mittelalters, Münster, 1908), Band VI, Heft 6, p. 32:

> L'idée que le monde désire Dieu est grecque et péripatéticienne. Dans un libre de la Métaphysique que S. Thomas a commenté, il lisait les paroles célèbres: "Movet autem sicut appetibile et intelligibile . . . movet autem ut amatum."

See also G. Combès, *La Charité d'après saint Augustin* (Paris, 1934), p. 257:

> Il semble bien ressortir de notre étude que la charité est le centre d'où rayonne toute la doctrine augustinienne. Elle inspire la théologie du grand docteur. Le "Deus caritas est" à la base et au sommet de ses expositions dogmatiques. C'est la charité substantielle de Dieu qui a engendré le Fils,

opéré la Procession du Saint-Esprit et constitué le lien éternel d'amour qui unit les trois personnes divines. C'est par charité que le Père a créé les hommes, par charité que le Fils s'est incarné pour endosser leurs misères, par charité qu'Il est mort sur la Croix pour racheter leurs iniquités; si bien que les trois grands mystères de la Sainte Trinité de l'Incarnation et de la Rédemption se résolvent dans un acte d'amour. Et cet amour de Dieu ne se contente pas d'agir pour nous de l'extérieur. Il pénètre dans nos âmes, diffusé par le Saint-Esprit, et nous fait participer sous une forme analogique mais vivante à la charité eternelle.

Page 61

Confessions, XIII, ix. The translation of this and all other passages quoted from the *Confessions* is that of Watts given in the Loeb Classical Library.

Page 61

Love known as charity. See Aquinas, *Summa theologica,* I-II, 26, 3.

We find four words referring, in a way, to the same things: viz., love, dilection, charity, and friendship. They differ, however, in this, that *friendship,* according to the Philosopher (Ethic. viii. 5) "is like a habit," whereas *love* and *dilection* are expressed by way of act or passion; and charity can be taken either way.

Moreover, these three express *act* in different ways. For love has a wider signification than the others, since every dilection or charity is love, but not vice versa. Because dilection implies, in addition to love, a choice (*electionem*) made beforehand, as the very word denotes; and therefore dilection is not in the concupiscible power, but only in the will, and only in the rational nature. . . Charity denotes, in addition to love, a certain perfection of love, in so far as that which is loved is held to be of great price, as the word itself implies *(carus).*

The translation is that of the Dominican Fathers, VI, 315.
See also Augustine, *De civitate Dei,* XIV, 7.

Page 61

Substantial love being the love of the Father for the Son and the love of the Son for the Father. One thinks at once, of course, of Dante's verses in *Paradiso,* x, 1-3:

> Guardando nel Suo figlio con l'Amore
> che l'uno e l'altro eternalmente spira,
> lo primo ed ineffabile valore.

And on this point see St. Augustine, *De trinitate,* XV, 19:

> Wherefore, if Holy Scripture proclaims that God is love, and that love is of God, and works this in us that we abide in God and He in us, and that hereby we know this, because He has given us of His spirit, then the Spirit Himself is God, who is love. Next, if there be among the gifts of God none greater than love, and there is no greater gift of God than the Holy Spirit, what follows more naturally than that He is Himself love, who is called both God and of God? And if the love by which the Father loves the Son and the Son loves the Father ineffably demonstrates the communion of both, what is more suitable than that He should be specially called love, who is the Spirit common to both?

The translation is that of Hadden in *Works of Augustine,* edited by Rev. M. Dods (Edinburgh, 1873), VII, 421.

Pages 62-63

St. Bernard, *De diligendo Deo,* edited by Williams and Mills (Cambridge University Press, 1926), chap. xii, pp. 60-61. Cf. E. Gilson, *La Théologie mystique de s. Bernard* (Paris, 1934), p. 118; also, "La Grâce et le saint Graal," in his volume *Les Idées et les lettres* (Paris, 1932), p. 63, on the meaning of the Grail. Gilson's fine distinctions there should help readers of the *Vita Nuova* with the same and similar problems.

In quoting the point from St. Bernard I mean, of course, to cite a typical statement of the matter. For Augustine, see note above to p. 61; also his *De trinitate,* XV, 32:

> Dilectio igitur quae ex Deo est et Deus est, proprie Spiritus sanctus est, per quem diffunditur in cordibus nostris Dei charitas, per quam nos tota inhabitat Trinitas. Quocirca rectissime Spiritus sanctus, cum sit Deus, vocatur enim Donum Dei. Quod Donum proprie quid nisi charitas intelligenda est, quae perducit ad Deum, et sine qua quodlibet aliud donum Dei non perducit ad Deum.

See also Aquinas, *Summa theologica,* II-II, 24, 2:

> Unde charitas non potest neque naturaliter nobis inesse, neque per vires naturales est acquisita, sed per infusionem Spiritus Sancti, qui est amor Patris et Filii, cuius participatio in nobis est ipsa caritas causata, sicut supra dictum est.

Cf. Guillaume de St. Thierry, *PL* 184, 387:

> Amor quippe illuminatus charitas est; amor a Deo, in Deo, ad Deum charitas est. Charitas autem Deus est . . . Brevis est laus, sed concludens

omnia. Quidquid de Deo potest dici, potest dici et de charitate; sic tamen ut, considerata secundum naturas doni et dantis, in dante nomen sit substantiae, in dato qualitatis.

Page 63

Augustine, *De doctrina christiana,* III, x (*PL* 34, 72):

Charitatem voco motum animi ad fruendum Deo propter ipsum, et se atque proximi propter Deum: cupiditatem autem, motum animi ad fruendum se et proximi et quolibet corpore non propter Deum.

The translation of this passage in the text is that of Shaw in *Nicene and Post-Nicene Fathers,* p. 561.

The passage on the distinction between *frui* and *uti* is found in *De doctrina christiana,* I, iv (*PL* 34, 20-21).

No thing, no creature, may rightly have terminal value in itself:

Aut sistitur in pulchritudine creaturae, aut per illam tenditur in aliud. Si primo modo tunc est via deviationis. (St. Bonaventura, I *Sententiarum,* 3, 1, un., 2, Quaracchi edition, t. I, p. 72.

For that is to stop short upon the road, as Augustine says (*De doctrina christiana,* I, 33):

Nam si in nobis id facimus, remanemus in via, et spem beatitudinis nostrae in homine vel in angelo collocamus.

Page 65

Truancy. I borrow the happy term from C. S. Lewis, *The Allegory of Love* (Oxford, 1936), a masterly study of the tradition of courtly love and of that same conflict between love of woman and love of God which, in my view, the *Vita Nuova* alone resolves without recantation. Lewis has followed out the theme of recantation from Andreas Capellanus to Chaucer's *Troylus* in such a penetrating way as to open up new perspectives in this regard for the student of the Spanish and Italian scenes. Only once does Lewis turn to the *Vita Nuova* and then he is, in my opinion, mistaken in his interpretation of its "allegory" (pp. 47-48). But this is a mere detail and must not prevent my acknowledgment here of the considerable debt which I owe to his fine study.

Three other studies touching on some of the same points as does Lewis contribute stimulating insights into the problem: Mme Lot-Borodine, "Sur les origines et les fins du service d'amour," *Mélanges de linguistique et de littérature offerts* à M. Alfred Jeanroy (Paris, 1928), pp. 223-242; Leo Spitzer, *L'Amour lointain de Jaufré Rudel et le sens de la poésie des troubadours* (University of North Carolina Studies in the Romance Languages and Literature, no 5; Chapel Hill, 1944); Gilson, *La Théologie mystique de s. Bernard,* pp. 193-215: "Saint Bernard et l'amour courtois."

Pages 65-66

Andreas Capellanus, *The Art of Courtly Love,* with introduction, translation, and notes by John Jay Parry (New York, 1941), pp. 187, 212. Or see the Latin text: Andreae Capellani, *De amore,* recensuit E. Trojel (Havniae, 1892), pp. 313-314, 360-361. The work is thought to have been written *c.* 1185.

Page 66

One third of the troubadours. J. Anglade, *Le Troubadour Giraut Riquier* (Paris, 1905), p. 283, n. l: "Lowinsky, par un calcul assez exacte, évalue à un tiers du nombre total des troubadours ceux dont nous savons qu'ils ont fini leur vie dans un cloître."

For Chaucer and Gower, see C. S. Lewis, *The Allegory of Love,* pp. 43, 218-220; Juan Ruiz, Arcipreste de Hita, *Libro de buen amor,* edited by Cejador, 2 vols. (Madrid, 1913). See the opening *oración* and the whole idea of the work as presented there (I, 1-14); and compare with the recantation of Andreas Capellanus cited above in the text.

Page 66

Petrarch. The first poem of the *Canzoniere* and *vanitas:*

> Voi ch'ascoltate in rime sparse il suono
> di quei sospiri ond'io nudriva 'l core
> in sul mio primo giovenile errore,
> quand'era in parte altr'uom da quel ch'i'sono,
>   del vario stile in ch'io piango e ragiono
> fra le vane speranze e'l van dolore,
> ove sia chi per prova intenda amore,
> spero trovar pietà, non che perdono.
>   Ma ben veggio or sì come al popol tutto
> favola fui gran tempo, onde sovente
> di me medesmo meco mi vergogno;

e del mio vaneggiar vergogna è 'l frutto,
e'l pentersi, e'l conoscer chiaramente
che quanto piace al mondo è breve sogno.

. . .

Padre del ciel, dopo i perduti giorni,
dopo le notti vaneggiando spese,
con quel fero desio ch'al cor s'accese,
mirando gli atti per mio mal sì adorni,
piacciati omai col tuo lume ch'io torni
ad altra vita, et a più belle imprese,
sì ch'avendo le reti indarno tese,
il mio duro adversario se ne scorni.
Or volge, Signor mio, l'undecimo anno
ch'i'fui sommesso al dispietato giogo,
che sopra i più soggetti è più feroce.
Miserere del mio non degno affanno;
reduci i pensier vaghi a miglior luogo;
ramenta lor come oggi fusti in croce.

Page 66

Petrarch's *Secretum,* otherwise known as *De contemptu mundi,* in *Opera omnia* (Basilea, 1581), I, 355:

Augustinus: Ab amore coelestium elongavit animum, et ab creatore ad creaturam desiderium inclinavit quae una quidem ad mortem pronior fuit via.

The Saint evidently takes his text from Romans (Vulg.) I, 24-25:

Propter quod tradidit illos Deus in desideria cordis eorum, in immunditiam; ut contumeliis afficiant corpora sua in semetipsis: qui commutaverunt veritatem Dei in mendacium, et coluerent et servierunt creaturae potius quam Creatori, qui est benedictus in saecula, amen.

The dialogue continues:

Francesco: Unum hoc (seu gratitudini seu ineptiae ascribendum) non sileo, me quantulumcumque conspicis, per illam esse, nec unquam ad hoc, si quid est nominis aut gloriae fuisse venturum, nisi virtutum tenuissimam sementem, quam pectore in hoc natura locaverat, nobilissimis his affectibus coluisset. Illa iuvenilem animum ab omni turpitudine revocavit, uncoque ut aiunt, retraxit, atque alta compulit spectare. Quid ni, certum enim est amorem in amatos mores transformare, atque nemo unquam tam mordax convitiator inventus est, qui huius famam canino dente contingeret,

qui dicere auderet (ne dicam in actibus eius, sed in gestu verborum) repre-
hensibile aliquid se vidisse. Ita qui nihil intactum liquerant, hanc mirantes,
venerantesque reliquerunt: minime igitur mirum est si haec tam celebris
fama, mihi quoque desiderium famae clarioris attulit, laboresque durissimos,
quibus optata consequerer mollivit. Quid enim adolescens aliud optabam
quam ut illi vel soli placerem, quae mihi vel sola placuerat. Quod ut mihi
contingeret spretis mille voluptatum illecebris, quod me ante tempis curis,
laboribusque subiecerim nosti, et iubes illam oblivisci vel partius amare, quae
me a vulgi consortio segregavit, quae dux viarum omnium, torpenti ingenio
calcar admonuit, ac semisopitum animum excitavit.

Compare Santa Lucia's words to Beatrice in *Inferno*, II, 103ff.:

> Disse: - Beatrice, loda di Dio vera,
>   chè non soccorri quei che t'amò tanto,
>   ch'uscì per te della volgare schiera?

Page 67

Recantation. It should be noted that Dante too, outside of the *Vita
Nuova,* makes his own recantation in keeping with the tradition: the
Convivio, in a sense, is that. See, too, his sonnet to Cino da Pistoia:

> Io mi credea del tutto esser partito
> da queste nostre rime, messer Cino,
> ché si conviene omai altro camino
> a la mia nave più lungi dal lito.

Page 68

Peace. See Augustine, *De civitate Dei,* XIX, 11:

Tantum est enim pacis bonum, ut etiam in rebus terrenis atque mortalibus
nihil gratius soleat audiri, nihil desiderabilius concupisci, nihil postremo possit melius inveniri.

Gilson, *L'Esprit de la philosophie médiévale,* p. 268:

Pax, mot magique pour une âme médiévale; rayonnant d'une lumière
égale et tranquille, il annonce le plus précieux et le moins accessible des biens.

Page 68

Summa theologica, I-II, 2, 8: *Utrum beatitudo hominis consistat in
aliquo bono creato.*

Respondeo. Dicendum quod impossibile est beatitudinem hominis esse in aliquo bono creato. Beatitudo enim est bonum perfectum, quod totaliter quietat appetitum; alioquin non esset ultimus finis, si adhuc restaret aliquid appetendum. Obiectum autem voluntatis, quae est appetitus humanus, est universale bonum; sicut obiectum intellectus est universale verum. Ex quo patet quod nihil potest quietare voluntatem hominis, nisi bonum universale. Quod non invenitur in aliquo creato, sed solum in Deo, quia omnis creatura habet bonitatem participatam. Unde solus Deus voluntatem hominis implere potest; secundum quod dicitur in Psalmo CII: "Qui replet in bonis desiderium" etc. In solo igitur Deo beatitudo hominis consistit.

Page 69

Historians of literature. See K. Vossler, for one, with his little volume, *Die philosophischen Grundlagen zum "süssen neuen Stil"* (Heidelberg, 1904). His thesis has been convincingly rejected by several scholars, but better than any by V. Rossi in his essay, "Dolce stil nuovo," in the miscellany *Le opere minori di Dante Alighieri* (Firenze, 1906), p. 75, n. 25. But, even though Rossi gave the proper rebuttal to Vossler here, he embraced nevertheless the thesis which I cannot accept; namely, that the *donna angelicata* of Guinicelli was a solution to the conflict between courtly love and love of God (*ivi*, p. 41):

> Sortito a vivere in un tempo di fede calda e sincera, quando il recente moto francescano aveva rinnovato d'intensità e d'intimità il sentimento religioso, e tuttavia sollevava turbe d'uomini a mistiche esaltazioni, il Guinicelli non poteva concepire quell'ardore virtuoso che nasceva in lui coll'amore, altrimenti che come ardore di virtù cristiane, come impulso ad operar nella vita quel bene morale, che segna la via la qual dirittamente conduce al Sommo Bene, a Dio, ultimo fine dell'uomo. L'amore per l'anima creata divenne quindi nella sua mente scala a salire verso la beatitudine celeste, e l'anima femminile che lo ispirava, guida all'amante verso l'amore del Bene "di là dal qual non è a che s'aspiri." Per tal guisa la donna senza perdere la sua individualità spirituale componeva, nel giudizio del poeta, il dissidio, assillo delle coscienze, tra l'umano e il divino; e l'amor della donna si conciliava coll'amore di Dio, senza che per questo fosse necessario cancellar lei dal novero delle cose amabili per sostituirle una astrazione intellettuale.

And Rossi proceeds to turn to the poem *Al cor gentil ripara sempre amore* as the chief support for these assertions. But here again, I repeat, he leaves us with a hazy idea of how this may be.

See also Mme Lot-Borodine, *Trois Essais sur le roman de Lancelot du Lac et la quête du saint Graal,* p. 4:

> Tel est bien le conflit tragique de tout le Moyen Age, sensuel et spiritualiste

en même temps, conflit qui ne se résout que plus tard dans un idéalisme
supérieur chez une élite, chez quelques poètes italiens du *dolce stil nuovo,*
poètes dont nous venons de nommer le plus grand [Dante]. Là seulement,
grâce à une haute inspiration mystique, l'antithèse deviendra une synthèse
ouvrant devant les élus une voie nouvelle, les conduisant jusqu'au Paradis par
la main de la *donna angelicata* de leurs rêves.

But it is high time that the *Vita Nuova* alone receive the credit for
being what it is, namely, the one and only solution to the conflict.

Page 70

    Praise of the beloved. Cf. *Convivio,* I, x, 6: "Dico che lo naturale
amore principalmente muove l'amatore a tre cose: l'una si è a magnificare
l'amato."

Page 70

    The text of the poems of Guido Guinicelli and Guido Cavalcanti cited
in the following pages (unless otherwise noted) is taken from the edition
Rimatori del dolce stil nuovo by Luigi Di Benedetto (Scrittori d'Italia;
Bari, 1939), and can be found there by the index of first verses.

Page 71

    The radiance that shines about her. The brightness belongs to the
donna angelicata and has religious implications everywhere which Dante,
for the most part, rendered explicit. Grace, in the *Divine Comedy,* is
made manifest in light:

Purgatorio, xiv, 78-80:

        Ma da che Dio in te vuol che *traluca*
          tanto sua grazia. . .

Paradiso, x, 82ff.:

        E dentro all'un senti' cominciar: "Quando
        lo raggio della grazia, onde s'accende
        verace amore e che poi cresce amando,

        multiplicato in te tanto resplende,
        che ti conduce su per quella scala.

But, as every student of Dante knows, there are many more passages to
be cited in this connection.

Page 71

The poet wounded to death by love. The theme finds its counter-part in mystic love of God. Its connections with and derivations from that conception of mystic love, the ecstatic, should be explored more carefully. Cf. Rousselot, *Pour l'histoire du problème de l'amour au moyen âge,* p. 65:

> Si l'amour est extatique et tire le sujet hors de soi, on se le représente naturellement comme un pouvoir destructeur, comme une force annihilatrice. Dans la conception physique l'amour était la chose du monde la plus profondément naturelle, l'expression même de l'essence en tendances. Ici il apparaît confusément comme contradictoire des appétits innés, comme un mouvement anti-naturel au premier chef. Aimer, dans l'école gréco-thomiste, c'est chercher son bien, c'est donc "trouver son âme," dans l'école extatique, c'est "la perdre." L'amour est ici une violence, c'est une "blessure," une "langueur," une "mort."

See also *ivi,* p. 4.

In the poems of Dante outside of the *Vita Nuova* there is no better example of the theme than his *canzone,* "Così nel mio parlar voglio esser aspro."

Page 74

The action begins with troubadour love. E. C. Gardner (*Dante and the Mystics* [London, 1913], pp. 9-10) observes the progression away from troubadour love in the *Vita Nuova* as follows:

> For, among the many things to which Dante is heir, he is heir to the troubadour tradition. Throughout the *Vita Nuova,* the perfect troubadour and the incipient mystic are reacting upon each other. . . And throughout the mystic is gradually absorbing the troubadour.

Page 75

For the question of Love as a substance or an accident as it appears in the tradition before Dante, see B. Nardi, "La Filosofia dell' amore," in his volume *Dante e la cultura medievale* (Bari, 1942), pp. 14ff. And see Cavalcanti's *canzone* beginning

> Donna me prega, perch'io voglio dire
> d'un accidente, che sovente è fero,
> ed è sì altero ch'è chiamato amore.

Page 76

The means by which the love of her lover is led back to God. See
Purgatorio, xxxi, 22-24, Beatrice speaking to Dante:

> Ond'ella a me: "Per entro i mie' disiri
> che ti menavano ad amar lo bene
> di là dal qual non è a che s'aspiri.

Page 76

The course of love like a circle. See also below, note to p. 103, and
Gilson, *L'Esprit de la philosophie médiévale,* p. 272:

> Éternellement préexistant dans le souverain bien, découlant de ce bien
> vers les choses par un acte de libre générosité, l'amour retourne au bien qui
> est son origine. Nous n'avons donc pas affaire ici avec un courant qui
> s'éloigne toujours plus de sa source, jusqu'à ce qu'enfin il se perde. Né de
> l'amour, l'univers créé est tout entier traversé, mu, vivifié du dedans, par
> l'amour qui circule en lui comme le sang dans le corps qu'il anime. Il y a
> donc une circulation de l'amour qui part de Dieu et y ramène.

In a treatise on love (of uncertain authorship) given in Migne,
Patrologie latine, vol. 184, col. 589, appears the following:

> Fames enim animae desiderium est. Sic vere Domini amans anima amore
> non satiatur: quia Deus amor est, quem qui amat, amorem amat. Amare
> autem amorem circulum facit, ut nullus finis sit amoris.

Page 77

A fair measure of the conceptual distance which separates the end
of the *Divine Comedy* from the end of the *Vita Nuova* is given by St.
Thomas' terms of *caritas viae* and *caritas patriae.* The *Vita Nuova,* to
the end, is concerned with a love which may be named by the first term.
And so, too, is the *Divine Comedy* (see *Paradiso,* ii, 22: *Beatrice in suso
e io in lei guardava*) until that moment comes when Beatrice steps aside
and is no longer medial between the poet and the vision of God; at that
moment the poem turns from *caritas viae* to *caritas patriae.* Cf. *Summa
theologica,* II-II, 24, 11 ad Resp.:

> Sed forma corporis caelestis, quia replet totam materiae potentialitatem,
> ita quod non remanet in ea potentia ad aliam formam, inamissibiliter inest.
> Sic igitur caritas patriae, quia replet totam potentialitatem rationalis mentis,
> inquantum scilicet omnis actualis motus eius fertur in Deum, inamissibiliter
> habetur. Caritas autem viae non sic replet potentialitatem sui subiecti, quia

non semper actu fertur in Deum. . . Ibi ergo caritas inamissibiliter habetur, ubi id quod convenit caritati non potest videri nisi bonum, scilicet in patria ubi Deus videtur per essentiam, quae est ipsa essentia bonitatis. Et ideo caritas patriae amitti non potest. Caritas autem viae, in cuius statu non videtur ipsa essentia Dei bonitatis esse essentia, potest amitti.

Or, see the terms *perfectio patriae* and *perfectio viae* which also apply in the same way (*Summa theologica*, II-II, 44, 4 ad Resp.)

Dicendum quod dupliciter contingit ex toto corde Deum diligere. Uno quidem modo in actu, idest ut totum cor hominis semper actualiter in Deum feratur. Et ista est perfectio patriae. Alio modo, ut habitualiter totum cor hominis in Deum feratur, ita scilicet quod nihil contra Dei dilectionem cor hominis recipiat. Et haec est perfectio viae.

Cf. also *ivi*, II-II, 44, 6.

Page 79

The special symmetrical arrangement of the poems. C. E. Norton, in the year 1859, was the first scholar to make public his observation of this symmetrical pattern. Twenty years earlier, however, Gabriele Rossetti had seen the essential outline of it, as is clear from a letter of his to Charles Lyell dated January 13, 1836. For this point and the whole history of the matter, see K. McKenzie, "The Symmetrical Structure of Dante's *Vita Nuova*," *Publications of the Modern Language Association*, XVIII (1903), 341ff. McKenzie (p. 350) considers the arrangement in terms of one and nine to be a mere ingenuity to which little importance should be attached. It had been suggested by Federzoni. But in A. Marigo, *Mistica e scienza nella Vita Nuova* (Padova, 1914), p. 85, n. 2, one finds further support for it; moreover, why should any pattern emphasizing the number nine in the *Vita Nuova* be of little importance?

Page 90

Richard of St. Victor, a mystic well known to Dante. See *Paradiso*, x, 130-132:

> Vedi oltre fiammeggiar l'ardente spiro
> d'Isidoro, di Beda e di Riccardo,
> che a considerar fu più che viro.

Epistola ad Canem Grandem, 420:

Et ubi ista invidis non sufficiant legant Richardum de Sancto Victore in libro *De Contemplatione*.

The quotation is from Richard's *Tractatus de gradibus charitatis,* *PL* 196, 1195. Mario Casella, for one, called Richard's words to the attention of Dante scholars some years ago (*Studi danteschi,* XVIII [1934], 108), and indicated their relevance to the problem of the *dolce stil nuovo.* And see B. Nardi, *Dante e la cultura medievale,* p. x.

Perhaps more of Richard's text than what has been given is relevant. The passage continues directly as follows:

Ne mireris igitur si alium audiere de ipsa mallem quam loqui ipse. Illum, inquam, audire vellem qui calamum linguae tingeret in sanguine cordis, quia tunc vera et veneranda doctrina est cum quod lingua loquitur conscientia charitas suggerit, et spiritus ingerit.

This latter figure in Richard and others seems to be inspired by Psalm XLIV (Vulg.):

Eructavit cor meum verbum bonum
dico ego opera mea regi.
Lingua mea calamus scribae
velociter scribentis.

For the idea of the "dictator," cf. *De monarchia,* III, ɪᴠ, 11.

Non enim peccatur in Moysen, non in David . . . sed in Spiritum Sanctum qui loquitur in illis. Nam quanquam scribe divini eloquii multi sint, unicus tamen dictator est Deus, qui beneplacitum suum nobis per multorum calamos explicare dignatus est.

And for the idea of the "inner" dictation, cf. Guillaume de St. Thierry, *De natura . . . amoris, PL* 184, 394:

Affectus ergo charitatis Deo indissolubiter inhaerens, et de vultu ejus omnia judicia sua colligens, ut agat vel disponat exterius, sicut voluntas Dei bona, et beneplacens, et perfecta dictat ei interius.

Page 91

Happiness in the contemplation of God and in praise of Him. See Aquinas, *Summa theologica,* II-II, 181, 4:

Respondeo. Dicendum quod, sicut supra dictum est, activa vita habet finem in exterioribus actibus; qui si referantur ad quietem contemplationis, iam pertinent ad vitam contemplativam. In futura autem vita beatorum cessabit occupatio exteriorum actuum; et si qui actus exteriores sint, referentur ad finem contemplationis. Ut enim Augustinus dicit in fine De Civit. Dei: "ibi vacabimus et videbimus; videbimus et amabimus; amabimus et laudabimus." Et in eodem libro praemittit quod ibi Deus "sine fine videbitur, sine fastidio amabitur, sine fatigatione laudabitur. Hoc munus, hic affectus, hic actus erit omnibus."

Page 91

Charity seeks no reward. See Augustine, *Enarratio in Psalmum LIII, PL* 36, 626:

Quia gratis amo quod laudo. Laudo Deum et in ipsa laude gaudeo: ipsius laude gaudeo . . . laudetur Deus noster voluntate, ametur charitate; gratuitum sit quod amatur et quod laudatur. Quid est gratuitum? Ipse propter se, non propter aliud. Si enim laudas Deum ut det tibi aliquid aliud, iam non gratis amas Deum.

I think there can be little doubt of the intentional analogy of the second stage of love in the *Vita Nuova* to this kind of love.

For love without hope of reward, see also St. Bernard, *De diligendo Deo,* chapter vii:

Non enim sine premio diligitur deus, etsi absque premii intuitu diligendus sit. Vacua namque vera caritas esse non potest, nec tamen mercennaria est. Quippe non querit que sua sunt. Affectus est non contractus, nec acquiritur pacto, nec acquirit. Sponte afficit, et spontaneum facit. Verus amor se ipso contentus est. Habet premium sed id quod amatur.

Page 93

Now that Bonagiunta is in Purgatory. I accept the interpretation of J. E. Shaw on this point ("Dante and Bonagiunta," *Report of the Dante Society* [Cambridge, Mass., April, 1936] pp. 6-7):

They [Dante's words *Io mi son un,* etc.] give Bonagiunta the cue that he has been waiting for, the chance to tell Dante what he has been longing to tell him, that now that he is no longer living he is a changed man; now that he is in Purgatory and on his way to Paradise he is at one with Dante in the knowledge of "Amore"; he sees now that it was ignorance of "Amore" that kept him and the other conventional poets from attaining to the sweet new style.

Shaw's arguments here (see pages following the above) for this understanding of Bonagiunta's "now" *(issa)* are, it seems to me, cogent enough.

I cannot, however, share Shaw's understanding of what the "sweet new style" is that Bonagiunta hears from Dante; for he takes it to be

in the *style* of the words *Io mi son un,* etc., whereas I cannot think it
to be anywhere except in the *concept* expressed by those words, a concept of love which, in the *Vita Nuova,* is put as the second stage of love,
a love which is already incipient charity.

Page 94

Love at the second stage a more noble matter. May one not hear, in
certain of the words which define love at the second stage, for example,
"lo mio segnore Amore, la sua merzede, ha posto tutta la mia *beati-*
tudine in quello che non mi puote venir meno," an echo of well-known
words spoken by Jesus to Martha who had complained that her sister
Mary sat at His feet all day while she was busied about the house: "Et
respondens dixit illi Dominus: Martha, Martha, sollicita es, et turbaris
erga plurima. Porro unum est necessarium. Maria optimam partem
elegit, *quae non auferetur ab ea"* (Luke [Vulg.] X, 41-42)? The echo is
faint enough, perhaps; too faint, indeed, for any such interpretation as
I have given to depend upon. It is not needed for that interpretation.
But in view of the analogy between the contemplative life (for which
Mary stood, of course) and the contemplative nature of the second stage
of love in the *Vita Nuova,* I venture to suggest that such an echo is not
illusory and that it, too, helps to say why the second stage is more noble
than the first: "Maria *optimam* partem elegit." Cf. Hugh of St. Victor,
PL 175, 816:

Martha, Martha. Repetitio nominis indicium est dilectionis, vel forte
movendae intentionis, ut audiret attentius. Non reprehenditur pars Marthae,
quia et ipsa bona, sed pars Mariae laudatur. Quae quare sit optima, subin-
fertur: *Quae non auferetur ab ea.* Quia contemplativa hic incipit, et in
coelesti patria perficitur; quia amoris ignis, qui ardere hic inchoat, eum ipsum
quem amat viderit, in amorem amplius ignescet. Non ergo contemplativa
auferetur: quae subtracta praesentis seculi luce perficitur.

Page 95

What if contemplation should be deprived of its object? See Beatrice to Dante, *Purgatorio,* xxxi, 49-54:

> Mai non t'appresentò natura o arte
>   piacer, quanto le belle membra in ch'io
>   richiusa fui, e sono in terra sparte;
>
> e se'l sommo piacer sì ti fallìo
>   per la mia morte, qual cosa mortale
>   dovea poi trarre te nel suo disio?

Pages 95-96

Final causes and the modern mind. One might, perhaps, date the end of our acceptance of final causes (as if that were possible!) from Spinoza's judgment upon them in his *Ethics,* Part I, Appendix: "Final causes are mere human figments." But every student of ancient and medieval thought knows how all important a consideration of final cause is in all attempts to understand phenomena. Of course, for Dante, Aristotle's understanding of the matter as expressed in the *Physics* (and the theologian's understanding of Aristotle) would in itself have sufficed to support the concept scientifically (religiously, it found an obvious support in the concept of God as *auctor naturae*):

Further, in any operation of human art, where there is an end to be achieved, the earlier and successive stages of the operation are performed for the purpose of realizing that end. Now, when a thing is produced by Nature, the earlier stages in every case lead up to the final development in the same way as in the operation of art, and vice versa. The operation is directed by a purpose; we may, therefore, infer that the natural process was guided by a purpose to the end that is realized. Thus, if a house were a natural product, the process would pass through the same stages that it in fact passes through when it is produced by art.

Indeed, as a general proposition, the arts either, on the basis of Nature, carry things further than Nature can, or they imitate Nature (*Physics,* II, viii [199a]. Loeb Classical Library, translated by Wicksteed).

See *De monarchia,* II, 7:

Rursus, cum in operabilibus principium et causa omnium sit ultimus finis . . . consequens est ut omnis ratio eorum quae sunt ad finem in ipso fine sumatur.

Page 98

The famous *canzone* of Cavalcanti is, of course, that beginning *Donna me prega.* Mario Casella has recently given what would appear to be the definitive critical edition of this poem in *Studi di filologia italiana,* VII (1944), 97ff. See at pages 132ff. his interpretation of the concept of love which the poem so obscurely expresses in its complicated internal rhymes. This study (because of the war) reached me after my essay was written; nor is this the place to follow out the necessarily intricate exegesis which it presents. Casella's general understanding of Cavalcanti's position in the "philosophy" of love as compared with that of Guinicelli and Dante is summarized (p. 159) as follows:

A differenza del Guinizelli e di Dante, che per amore dell'oggetto contemplato e considerato in se stesso lasciano scaturire l'azione dalla sovrabbondanza della contemplazione, il Cavalcanti resta chiuso in se stesso: uomo della pura natura. E perciò fuori dell'ordine della moralità cristiana, per la quale l'amore, che ci introduce nel regno dei fini, è finalizzato tutto intero dalla visione beatifica e dall'amore di Dio, preso in se stesso e al di sopra di ogni cosa. Un amore che si perfeziona mediante le virtù morali e intellettuali e, nella vita soprannaturale—la vita della carità che ci connaturalizza a Dio—si orienta e si ordina tutto verso l'eterno mediante le virtù teologali e i doni.

I hope it is clear from my own brief treatment how entirely I agree with the distinction as regards Dante and Cavalcanti; and likewise how I disagree as regards Dante and Guinicelli since, in my view, the latter too, as one who keeps to the tradition of courtly love, is "fuori dell'ordine della moralità cristiana" and in conflict with it just as Petrarch was in singing of Laura as the terminus of all desire.

Page 100

The Vita Nuova written first of all for Guido Cavalcanti.   That this is the case, we know of course from the text: "E simile intenzione so ch'ebbe questo mio primo amico a cui io ciò scrivo, cioè ch'io li scrivessi solamente volgare" (last words of chapter xxx).   Too little attention has been paid to this clear statement on the part of the author.   Not that the *Vita Nuova* is written *only* for the "first friend."   It is also addressed to all those (and they are never many!) who have *intelletto d'amore.*

Page 103

A love which first moved from Heaven and which lifts from there. See Thomas Aquinas, *Summa theologica,* I-II, 26, 2 ad Resp.:

Nam appetitivus motus circulo agitur, ut dicitur in III De Anima; appetibile enim movet appetitum, faciens quodammodo in eo eius intentionem et appetitus tendit in appetibile realiter consequendum, ut sit ibi finis motus ubi fuit principium.

Compare *Purgatorio,* xvi, 85-90:

> Esce di mano a lui che la vagheggia
> prima che sia, a guisa di fanciulla
> che piangendo e ridendo pargoleggia,

l'anima semplicetta che sa nulla,
salvo che, mossa da lieto fattore,
volentier torna a ciò che la trastulla.

Thomas Aquinas also uses the figure of the Archer to illustrate the movement of Providence which disposes things toward their end (*Summa theologica*, I, 23 ad Resp.). See also note to p. 114 above.

Page 104

Death takes Beatrice away. Just so, charity of the way may be temporarily lost. See Thomas Aquinas, *Summa theologica*, II-II, 24, 11 (Dominican Fathers' translation, IX, 301-302):

Whereas the charity of the wayfarer does not so fill the potentiality of its subject, because the latter is not always directed to God: so that where it is not actually directed to God, something may occur whereby charity is lost. . . Therefore the charity of heaven cannot be lost, whereas the charity of the way can, because in this state God is not seen in His essence, which is the essence of goodness.

Page 104

The lover thrown back upon himself and his own free will.

"L'homme déchu possède une volonté capable de vouloir, mais incapable de vouloir le bien; la grâce est un don de Dieu qui nous remet en état de le vouloir" (Gilson, *Les Idées et les lettres,* p. 65, giving the thought of St. Bernard on this point).

Page 104

A will which up to this point had been bound in love of her. Not enough attention had been paid to this fact in the interpretation of the *Vita Nuova.* Love for Beatrice is not the result of a choice. Love for her is a passion. It is from the first an irresistible power from a source above the reaches of reason, though of course in accord with reason. In this connection the following point in Thomas Aquinas' *Summa theologica* (I-II, 26, 3) seems relevant:

Dicendum quod ideo aliqui posuerunt etiam in ipsa voluntate nomen amoris esse divinius nomine dilectionis, quia amor importat quandam passionem, praecipue secundum quod est in appetitu sensitivo; dilectio autem praesupponit iudicium rationis. Magis autem in Deum homo potest tendere per amorem passive quodammodo ab ipso Deo attractus, quam ad hoc eum propria ratio possit ducere. . . Et propter hoc divinius est amor quam dilectio.

It would not have been possible for the will to resist Beatrice who is beatitude:

Et quia defectus cuiuscumque boni habet rationem non boni, ideo illud solum bonum quod est perfectum et cui nihil deficit, *est tale bonum quod voluntas non potest non velle; quod est beatitudo* (*ivi*, I-II, 10, 2 ad Resp.).

Page 105

A mystic tradition. See especially on this point Gilson, *La théologie mystique de s. Bernard*, pp. 108ff., and the work of Gardner cited below.

Page 105

Song of degrees. Cf. Psalms 122-134.

Page 105

Purgative, illuminative, unitive. See Gardner, *Dante and the Mystics*, p. 90:

Threefold is this way to God, to wit, first, the purgative way, whereby the mind is disposed to learn true wisdom. The second way is called the illuminative, whereby the mind by pondering is kindled to the burning of love. The third, the unitive, whereby the mind, above all understanding, reason and intellect, is directed upwards to God alone.

The mystic theology of the Pseudo-Dionysius is the source for this terminology and these degrees.

Page 106

Thomas Aquinas, *Summa contra gentiles*, IV, ɪ.

Page 106

The true mystic. For the use of terms which would seem to describe an order of knowledge when actually they describe an order of love, see Gilson, "La Grâce et le saint Graal," in his volume *Les idées et les lettres*, pp. 88-89:

Reste, il est vrai, à éxpliquer l'emploi de la terminologie dont use ce roman pour décrire l'extase et qui suggère immédiatement l'interprétation que l'on en a proposée. Comment ne pas prendre en leur sens littéral des termes tels que *voir ouvertement, regarder, connaître?* Mais d'abord, s'ils signifiaent un idéal de connaissance intellectuelle, nous devrions renoncer de toute façon à maintenir le caractère cistercien de l'oeuvre. . . Or, il se trouve qu'en fait, l'école mystique de Cîteaux a pour caractère propre de désigner par des formules cognitives des états essentiellement affectifs. . . Une perspective historique commode pour saisir le caractère distinctif de cette doctrine est l'opposition bien connue entre la conception augustinienne et la conception thomiste de la Béatitude. Pour les augustiniens et les cisterciens, qui sont des affectifs, c'est la jouissamce de Dieu par l'amour qui constitue la béatitude; pour les thomistes, qui sont des intellectualistes, c'est la connaissance de Dieu par l'intelligence qui est la béatitude, l'amour de Dieu ne faisant qu'en résulter.

Gilson's distinctions here could be brought into Dante studies with great profit. All students of the *Divine Comedy* would then agree, I think, that in that great poem the two ways, the way of knowledge and the way of love, are fused. But must we not recognize that the dialectic of the *Vita Nuova* is a dialectic of the way of *love* and only that? And with such recognition is it not also clear that those scholars who, like K. Vossler, have tried to force it (and the *donna angelicata*) to be the solution to a problem in the order of *knowledge* have done much to distort our view of the work and of the *dolce stil nuovo*. Dante himself, as he looks back on the *Vita Nuova* from the intellectual position of the *Convivio,* sees it as *fervida* and *appassionata*.

And having recognized that the *Vita Nuova* is about a love which may be also called charity, we should do well to remember that charity is in an appetitive power. Thomas Aquinas, *Summa theologica,* II-II, 26, 1:

Faith pertains to the cognitive power, whose operation depends on the thing known in the knower. On the other hand, charity is in an appetitive power, whose operation consists in the soul tending to things themselves.

Note also, at II-II, 24, 9 of the *Summa theologica,* the distinction of three degrees of charity.

Page 107

Love ordered toward an end and the three stages. See Gilson, *La Philosophie de s. Bonaventure,* p. 429 (giving the Saint's position):

Elle [la grâce] tombe donc sur le libre arbitre et les facultés qui en dépendent. Dès qu'elle s'en est emparée, la grâce les ordonne en situant chacune d'elles à la place qu'elle doit occuper et en réglant son activité comme elle doit l'être pour que l'âme se trouve ramenée à Dieu. Trois opérations principales définissent, en effet, la vie de l'âme considérée sous sa forme la plus haute: chercher Dieu hors de soi, le chercher en soi, le chercher enfin au-dessus de soi.

Gilson here has in mind the following passage from St. Bonaventura's *In Hexaëmeron* (Quaracchi edition of *Opera omnia*, t. V, p. 442):

Tertio modo modus distinguendi in anima secundum *regressum* est secundum triplicem gradum contemplationis. Gregorius super Ezechielem (Libr. II homil. 5, n. 8ff.) ponit tres gradus: aut enim quod venit in considerationem nostram est *extra* nos, aut *intra* nos, aut *supra* nos.

Page 107

My citations from St. Bonaventura's *Itinerarium mentis in Deum* are from the text given in vol. V of the *Opera omnia*, Ad Claras Aquas (Quaracchi, 1891), pp. 295ff. The first words after the Prologue give the fundamental text for the three stages in the Saint's pattern of the ascent to God:

Chap. I. *De gradibus ascensionis in Deum et de speculatione ipsius per vestigia eius in universo.*

1. *Beatus vir, cuius est auxilium abs te, ascensiones in corde suo disposuit in valle lacrymarum, in loco, quem posuit.* Cum beatitudo nihil aliud sit, quam summi boni fruitio; et summum bonum sit supra nos: nullus potest effici beatus, nisi supra semetipsum ascendat, non ascensu corporali, sed cordiali. Sed supra nos levari non possumus nisi per virtutem superiorem nos elevantem. . .

2. Cum enim secundum statum conditionis nostrae ipsa rerum universitas sit scala ad ascendendum in Deum; et in rebus quaedam sint *vestigium,* quaedam *imago,* quaedam *corporalia,* quaedam *spiritualia,* quaedam *temporalia,* quaedam *aeviterna,* ac per hoc quaedam *extra nos,* quaedam *intra nos:* ad hoc, quod perveniamus ad primum principium considerandum, quod est *spiritualissimum* et *aeternum* et *supra nos,* oportet nos *transire* per *vestigium,* quod est *corporale* et *temporale* et *extra nos,* et hoc est *deduci in via Dei;* oportet, nos *intrare* ad mentem nostram, quae est *imago Dei aeviterna, spiritualis* et *intra nos,* et hoc est *ingredi in veritate Dei;* oportet, nos *transcendere* ad aeternum, spiritualissimum, et *supra nos,* aspiciendo ad primum principium, et hoc est *laetari in Dei notitia et reverentia maiestatis.*

The passage cited in the text occurs on p. 297, cols. 1-2. For the three stages in St. Augustine, see F. Cayré *La Contemplation d'après saint Augustin* (Paris, 1927), pp. 201 ff: "Les trois étapes."

Page 108

That blessed half hour when there is silence in Heaven. Richard of St. Victor, *Tractatus de quatuor gradibus violentae charitatis, PL* 196, 1220:

Tertius itaque amoris gradus est quando mens hominis in illam rapitur divini lumini abyssum, ita ut humanus animus in hoc statu exteriori omnium oblitus penitus nesciat seipsum totusque transeat in Deum suum et faciat quod scriptum est: Etenim non credentes inhabitare Dominum Deum (Psal. LXVII). In hoc itaque statu plene compescitur, profundeque sopitur carnalium desideriorum turba, et fit in coelo silentium quasi hora dimidia.

Apocalypsis B. Joannis, VIII, 7: *Factum est silentium in coelo quasi dimidia hora.*

Page 109

St. Bonaventura's third stage: *Itinerarium mentis in Deum* (see note to page 107 above), p. 297.

Page 109

For St. Augustine, *mens* is the uppermost part of the human soul, and St. Bonaventura is of course aware of that in using the term. See E. Gilson, *Introduction à l'étude de s. Augustin* (Paris, 1943):

En fait, il n'y a rien dans la nature qui ne porte quelque ressemblance de la Trinité et ne puisse par conséquent nous aider à la concevoir; toutefois, prise en son sens propre, la dignité d'image n'appartient qu'à l'homme; dans l'homme elle n'appartient en propre qu'à la pensée—*mens*—qui en est la partie supérieure *et la plus proche de Dieu.*

It is that latter fact (my italics) which ought to seem relevant to the use of *mente* in the *Vita Nuova*. See Gilson's references and notes to the above point. See also *Convivio*, III, ɪɪ, 10-19.

Page 110

One of the greatest mystics is St. Bernard. These words of his occur in *In cantica canticorum*, sermo III, 1 (*PL* 183, 794). On this point, see Gilson, *La théologie mystique de s. Bernard*, p. 116:

Saint Bernard a plusieurs fois repris la description de ces transformations unifiantes et de ces assimilations progressives. Il est assez difficile de dire si les états mystiques se classent chez lui selon une hiérarchie définie, et quelle elle pourrait être. Les deux principes auxquels il tient fermement, sont la supériorité des états purement "spirituels" sur ceux où les images jouent encore un rôle, et le caractère essentiellement divers, sans commune mesure, des expériences mystiques individuelles . . . seule l'expérience peut nous faire connaître ce que sont de tels états, et l'expérience de l'un ne vaut pas pour l'autre: à chacun de boire l'eau de son propre puits.

Gilson here cites the words I have given (*Hodie legimus,* etc.).   See also page 131, where Gilson touches again on the point of view of the mystic

qui se raconte, se penche sur sa propre existence, pour essayer de dire ce qui se passe en lui, comme saint Bernard va le faire pour nous.

In *PL* 184, 624 (a work not by St. Bernard), one finds the phrase *Saepe in libro experientiae legimus.*

Page 113

The analogy. Strictly speaking and in established terms, the analogy of Beatrice and *salute* through her, to Christ and *salute* through Him, is an analogy *of proportion,* not of proportionality, since both ways reach the same goal: the same salvation, the same living Christian God.   One action is not independent of the other, but that involving Beatrice is contained within, is subsumed by, that larger one involving Christ; it finds its validity by the light of that larger action.

For the whole matter of analogy, so vital to Christian theology, see B. Landry, *La Notion d'analogie chez saint Bonaventure et saint Thomas d'Aquin* (Louvain, 1922); G. B. Phelan, *St. Thomas and Analogy* (Milwaukee, 1941); also Gilson, *La Philosophie de s. Bonaventure,* pp. 201ff., for an analysis of this fundamental point in that philosophy ("l'analogie est la loi selon laquelle s'est effectuée la création . . . c'est la structure même de l'univers que nous habitons, c'est notre propre structure qui se trouvent ici en jeu").

Also see Gilson's remarks (*L'Esprit de la philosophie médiévale,* p. 136), concluding,

D'un mot, de même que l'être créé est un analogue de l'être divin [with St. Thomas] la causalité créée est un analogue de la causalité créatrice.

This, too, seems a relevant measure of the relation of the *salute* brought by Beatrice to the *salute* brought by Christ.

Page 114

For Dante as poet of the "rightness of the will," *directio voluntatis* or *rectitudo,* see his own evaluation of himself as such in his *De vulgari eloquentia,* II, ii, 8-9.   It was Cino da Pistoia, not himself, whom Dante saw as preëminent in the matter of love (*amoris accensio*).

Page 115

The reflective movement in the Book of Memory. In St. Bonaventura's *Itinerarium mentis in Deum* (V, 303), one comes across a conception of memory as that place where the reflective movement of understanding (such as might be represented by a gloss in the Book of Memory) would properly take place:

> Quia nihil capimus per intelligentiam, quod non sit praesens apud nos-
> tram memoriam.

And he continues:

> Operatio autem memoriae est retentio et representatio non solum *praesen-
> tium, corporalium* et *temporalium* verum etiam *succedentium, simplicium* et
> *sempiternalium.*—Retinet namque memoria *praeterita* per recordationem,
> *praesentia* per susceptionem, *futura* per praevisionem.

This can help a modern reader to realize that much more may take
place in the memory than he ordinarily conceives of. St. Bonaventura's
notion of the memory harks back, of course, to St. Augustine's—for
which see especially Book X of the *Confessions* (*venio in campos et
lata praetoria memoriae*), where one learns that God may inhabit the
memory and be sought out there and found. On St. Augustine's doctrine of the memory, see J. Guitton, *Le temps et l'éternité chez Plotin
et Saint Augustin* (Paris, 1933), pp. 199ff. For our own conclusions
stressing the analogy of Beatrice in the memory to that of Christ, certain of M. Guitton's remarks here are of extreme interest, for example,
pp. 203-204:

> Entre la vision et le souvenir, saint Augustin hésitera. La connaissance
> que nous avons de Dieu dans la vie présente est improprement définie par
> le terme de vision, parce qu'entre Dieu et l'âme il n'y a pas de commune
> mesure; si certains ont vu Dieu, c'est dans sa propre lumière et par la force
> qu'il a mise en eux. On ne peut l'appeler mémoire au sens moderne; car
> ce n'est pas le passé qu'elle atteint mais l'intimité du présent. Néanmoins
> pour saint Augustin la connaissance de Dieu est beaucoup plus mémoire que
> vision.

This is *memoria Dei,* of which M. Guitton says (p. 208):

> La memoria Dei soumet au temps la connaissance de l'immuable: c'est
> ainsi que Dieu a une histoire en nous.

> C'est histoire, en un sens, ce sont les *Confessions* tout entières.

Cf also Combès, *La Charité d'après s. Augustin,* p. 157:

C'est donc que notre mémoire s'étend par delà les limites de la psychologie jusqu'aux derniers sommets de la métaphsique. Dieu y habite réellement.

See as one sample from Book X of the *Confessions* (pp. xxiv ff.):

Ecce quantum spatiatus sum in memoria mea quaerens te, domine, et non te inveni extra eam. Neque enim aliquid de te inveni, quod non meminissem, ex quo didici te. Nam ex quo didici te, non sum oblitus tui. Ubi enim inveni veritatem, ibi inveni deum meum, ipsam veritatem, quam ex quo didici, non sum oblitus. Itaque ex quo te manes in memoria mea, et illic te invenio, cum reminiscor tui et delector in te. Hae sunt sanctae deliciae meae, quas donasti mihi misericordia tua respiciens paupertatem meam.

Sed ubi manes in memoria mea, domine, ubi illic manes? Quale cubile fabricasti tibi? Quale sanctuarium aedificasti tibi? Tu dedisti hanc dignationem memoriae mae, ut maneas in ea, sed in qua eius parte maneas, hoc considero . . . et dignatus es habitare in memoria mea ex quo te didici.

Et quid quaero, quo loco eius habites, quasi vero loca ibi sint? Habitas certe in ea, quoniam tui memini, ex quo te didici, et in ea te invenio, cum recordor te.

Page 115

The reflection of the eternal idea of Christ. Cf. Dante, *Epistola ad Canem Grandem,* 56:

. . . erit devenire ad primum, qui Deus est. Et sic, mediate vel inmediate, omne quod habet esse, habet esse ab eo; quia ex eo quod causa secunda recipit a prima, influit super causatum ad modum recipientis et reddentis radium.

Ivi, 60:

Propter quod patet quod omnis essentia et virtus procedat a prima, et intelligentie inferiores recipiant quasi a radiante, et reddant radios superioris ad suum inferius ad modum speculorum. Quod satis aperte tangere videtur Dionysius De Celesti Hierarchia loquens.

Paradiso, xiii, 52-54:

> Ciò che non more e ciò che può morire
> non è se non splendor di quella idea
> che partorisce, amando, il nostro sire.

Page 115

The touchstone by which its reality as good love can be known. Cf. *Paradiso,* iv, 124-128:

Io veggio ben che già mai non si sazia
nostro intelletto, se'l ver non lo illustra
di fuor dal qual nessun vero si spazia.

Posasi in esso come fera in lustra,
tosto che giunto l'ha; e giugner pòllo.

This measure of a lower reality by a higher one is a pattern which
Christian philosophy inherited, of course, from Greek philosophy (Plato,
Aristotle, Neoplatonism). Cf. W. H. Inge, *The Philosophy of Plotinus*
(London, 1923), I, 127:

> In other words, the explanation of a thing must always be sought in
> what is above it in the scale of value and existence, not in what is below.
> The higher does not need the lower, but the lower does need the higher.

The touchstone, needless to say, vouches for the beauty as well as
the goodness of the love for Beatrice, as may readily be seen through
words of Menéndez y Pelayo, *Historia de las ideas estéticas en España,*
chap. v, Introduction:

> No vino a enseñar estética ni otra ninguna ciencia humana el Verbo En-
> carnado; pero presentó en su persona y en la union de sus dos naturalezas
> el prototipo más alto de la hermosura, y el objeto más adecuado del amor,
> lazo entre los cielos y la tierra.

Pages 115-116

Renovatur de die in diem. Cf. also the pertinent phrase in Romans
(Vulg.) VI, 4: *ita et nos in novitate vitae ambulemus.* One should also
remember *Convivio,* III, viii, 20, where Dante glosses his *canzone* with
the words, "a dare ad intendere che la sua bellezza [of this Lady] ha
podestade in *rinnovare* natura in coloro che la mirano; *ch'è miracolosa
cosa.*"

Degrees or stages in the life of love are conceivable because of the
gradual increase of that love which is charity, as provided for, for example, by Thomas Aquinas (*Summa theologica* II-II, 24, 4, translated
by the Dominican Fathers, IX, 285):

> The charity of a wayfarer can increase. For we are called wayfarers by
> reason of our being on the way to God, who is the last end of our happiness.
> In this way we advance as we get nigh to God, who is approached "not by
> steps of the body but by the affections of the soul" (St. Augustine, *Tract. in
> Joan,* xxxii), and this approach is the result of charity, since it unites man's
> mind to God. Consequently it is essential to the charity of a wayfarer that

it can increase, for if it could not, all further advance along the way would cease.

And further on here (in words which the reader will recognize as relevant, remembering that love is an accident):

> For since charity is an accident, its being is to be in something. . .
> Hence charity increases essentially, not by beginning anew or ceasing to be in its subject . . . but by beginning to be more and more in its subject.

Nor is this all. St. Augustine's notion of the memory allowing for God to reside there allows also for the gradual revelation there (as in the Book of Memory) of the presence of mysteries. See on this Combès, *La Charité d'après s. Augustin,* p. 155:

> Notre mémoire n'est donc pas seulement un souvenir du passé, elle est la conscience du présent et d'un présent qui lui révèle tour les jours un peu plus ses incalculables richesses . . . ce ne sont pas, en effet, comme l'a cru Platon, des connaissances acquises dans une autre vie et qui peu à peu, sous l'effort de notre pensée s'actualisent. C'est le Verbe eternel qui, par ses faisceaux de lumière, nous découvre à tout instant d'immenses échappées sur la verité.

Page 116

What the Middle Ages would consider to be form. Cf. J. Maritain, *Art et scolastique* (3rd ed.; Paris, 1935), p. 38:

> *Splendor formae,* disait saint Thomas [of beauty] dans son langage précis de métaphysicien: car la "forme," c'est-à-dire le principe qui fait la perfection propre de tout ce qui est, qui constitue et achève les choses dans leur essence et dans leurs qualités, qui est enfin, si l'on peut ainsi parler, le secret ontologique qu'elles portent en elles, leur être spirituelle, leur mystère opérant, est avant tout le principe propre d'intelligibilité, la clarté propre de toute chose. Aussi bien toute forme est-elle un vestige ou un rayon de l'Intelligence créatrice imprimé au coeur de l'être créé.

But a student of Dante, as usual, will have to go no further than Dante for this idea in one of its most impressive statements and realizations: with the Eagle of *Paradiso,* xviii, and especially with the verses (106-111):

> E quietata ciascuna [favilla] in suo loco,
> la testa e'l collo d'un'aguglia vidi
> rappresentare a quel distinto foco.

Quei che dipinge lì, non ha chi'l guidi;
ma esso guida, e da lui si rammenta
quella virtù ch'è forma per li nidi.

Page 116

As we read that hymn. The whole of the hymn is to be found in
PL 184, 1317ff.; and in the *Oxford Book of Mediaeval Verse,* although
with some questionable alterations in the text, notably in the famous
first verse. For a discussion of the text itself and the questionable
attribution to St. Bernard, see R. Vaux, "Jesu dulcis memoria," *The
Church Quarterly Review* (1929), pp. 120-125, and Gilson's excellent
study, "La Mystique Cistercienne et le Iesu dulcis memoria," in his
volume, *Les Idées et les lettres;* also, more recently, A. Wilmart, *Le
"Jubilus" dit de S. Bernard* (Rome, 1944). I give below only those
stanzas of the hymn which seem most relevant to the analogy which I
wish to point out:

> Jesu dulcis memoria
> Dans vera cordi guadia:
> Sed super mel et omnia
> Ejus dulcis praesentia.
>   Nil canitur suavius,
>   Nil auditur jucundius,
>   Nil cogitatur dulcius,
>   Quam Jesus Dei Filius.

. . .

>   Jesu dulcedo cordium!
> Fons vivus, lumen mentium,
> Excedens omne gaudium,
> Et omne desiderium.
>   Nec lingua valet dicere,
> Nec littera exprimere:
> Expertus potest credere,
> Quid sit Jesum diligere.

. . .

>   Jesu rex admirabilis:
> Et triumphator nobilis,
> Dulcedo ineffabilis
> Totus desirabilis.
>   Mane nobiscum Domine

Et nos illustra lumine,
Pulsa mentis caligine,
Mundum replens dulcedine.
    Quando cor nostram visitas,
Tunc lucet ei veritas,
Mundi vilescit vanitas,
Et intus fervet charitas.
    Amor Jesu dulcissimus
Et vere suavissimus,
Plus millies gratissimus,
Quam dicere sufficimus
    Hoc probat ejus Passio,
Hoc sanguinis effusio,
Per quam nobis redemptio
Datur, et Dei visio.

    .   .   .

    Jesu mi bone, sentiam,
Amoris tui copiam,
Da mihi per praesentiam
Tuam videre gloriam.

    .   .   .

    Tu fons misericordiae,
Tu verae lumen patriae:
Pelle nubem tristitiae,
Dans nobis lucem gloriae.

More recently, in his *Théologie mystique de s. Bernard,* pp. 104-105, M. Gilson has summarized the conclusions of the above essay as follows:

Ce texte, du même chapitre III [of St. Bernard's *De diligendo deo*], sert d'introduction à cette idée très importante, que la *memoria,* entendons par lá la mémoire, le souvenir sensible de la passion du Christ, est en nous la condition et l'annonce de la *praesentia,* c'est-a-dire, au sens plein, de la vision béatifique dans la vie future, mais aussi déjà de ces visitations de l'âme par le Verbe en cette vie. "Dei ergo quaerentibus et suspirantibus *praesentiam,* presto interim et dulcis memoria est, non tamen qua satientur, sed qua magis esuriant unde satientur." On voit assez par tout le contexte qu'il s'agit ici de la *memoria passionis.* Celui qui trouve pénible le souvenir fréquent de la passion, comment soutiendra-t-il la présence du Verbe venant en juge? "Verbum modo crucis audire gravatur ac *memoriam passionis* sibi judicat onerosam; verum qualiter verbi illius pondus *in praesentia* sustinebit?" Il en va tout au contraire de celui à qui le souvenir de la passion est cher et familier. "Ceterum fidelis anima et suspirat *praesentiam* inhianter et in *memoria* requiescit suaviter." Nous rencontrons donc ici un thème théologique, devenu célèbre dans l'histoire de la poésie latine du moyen âge, grâce au fameux *Jesu dulcis memoria.* On voit en même temps que si ce poème n'a pas été écrit par saint Bernard lui-même, il dépend étroitement de son influence et exprime l'un des aspects les plus importants de sa doctrine mystique. Chose plus utile encore, on peut désormais lui donner son sens exact. Il décrit le mouvement par lequel l'âme s'élève du souvenir de la passion du Christ à l'union mystique, en attendant qu'elle lui soit unie pour toujours dans l'éternité.

I hardly need say, of course, that I claim no influence of the *Jesu dulcis memoria* on the *Vita Nuova.* But what I do wish to point out is precisely that "theological theme" of which the one is an expression and the other, inscribed in a Book of Memory, is an analogue.